THE INDUSTRIAL C
1820–1870

CONTEXT AND COMMENTARY

Series Editor: ARTHUR POLLARD

THE INDUSTRIAL CITY
1820–1870

Dorothy and Alan Shelston

MACMILLAN

First published 1990

Published by
MACMILLAN EDUCATION LTD
Houndmills, Basingstoke, Hampshire RG21 2XS
and London
Companies and representatives
throughout the world

Typeset by Wessex Typesetters
(Division of The Eastern Press Ltd)
Frome, Somerset.

Printed in Hong Kong

British Library Cataloguing in Publication Data
Shelston, Dorothy
The industrial city, 1820–1870.—(Context and
commentary)
1. Great Britain. Urban regions, history
I. Title II. Shelston, Alan III. Series
941'.009'732

ISBN 0–333–39494–1
ISBN 0–333–39572–7 pbk

Contents

List of Plates

1. *Manchester*, 1843. Photograph courtesy of the Central Library, Manchester.

2. 'Manchester, Getting up the Steam', from *The Builder*, 1853. Photograph courtesy of the Central Library, Manchester.

3. Rodney-Street, Liverpool. Photograph courtesy of Liverpool City Libraries.

4. Birmingham: a Working-Class Court. Photograph © Birmingham City Council Public Libraries Department.

5. Policemen in Manchester, *c.* 1850–60. Photograph courtesy of the Manchester Police Museum.

6. Leeds Town Hall, 1858. Photograph © Leeds City Council.

Acknowledgements

We should like to acknowledge the help we have received from the staff of the various Manchester libraries: most notably the John Rylands University Library of Manchester, the City of Manchester Central Library, and the Portico Library, and in particular its librarian, Mrs Janet Allan. The illustration of the Manchester Police Force is by courtesy of the Manchester Police Museum, and we should like to thank the museum's curator, Mr Duncan Broady, for his help with this and other matters. As in all projects of this kind, we are conscious of our indebtedness to conversations with friends and colleagues too numerous to mention, but we want in particular to thank Dr Michael Rose of the Department of History, University of Manchester, for reading two of our chapters in draft, and for his advice on matters of detail. Finally we thank Professor Arthur Pollard, General Editor of this series, for his encouragement and, even more, for his very considerable patience over a far longer haul than he can have anticipated.

The author and publishers wish to thank the following for permission to use copyright material: Basil Blackwell Ltd. for material from F. Engels, *The Condition of the Working Class in England* (1845), translated and edited by W. O. Henderson and W. H. Chaloner, 1971; J. P. Mayer for material from Alexis de Tocqueville, *Journeys to England and Ireland*, translated by G. Laurence and K. P. Mayer (Faber and Faber, 1958); Thames and Hudson Ltd. for material from Hippolyte Taine, *Notes on England*, translated by Edward Hyams, 1957. Every effort has been made to trace all the copyright holders but if any have been inadvertently overlooked the publishers will be pleased to make the necessary arrangement at the first opportunity.

A Note on References

The date of the original publication of all works cited is given on the first occasion on which they appear. In the case of works which have been frequently reprinted – notably, but not exclusively, novels – we have given chapter rather than page references. Full details of all works cited are given in the bibliography.

Authors' Preface

To contemporary observers, the towns and cities that grew out of the Industrial Revolution were a dramatically new phenomenon. As such, they evoked a variety of excited comment: there is no shortage of historical or literary documentation to convey to us the nature of this novel experience. In this volume we have attempted to record some of these reactions, and to bring together a selection of the extensive commentary on the experience of life within the cities during the period of their expansion in the early and middle years of the nineteenth century.

The more we have become acquainted with this original material the more has been revealed to us the complexity of our subject. We have taken as our title 'The Industrial City', explicitly excluding those cities – notably, but not only, London – that lie beyond the immediate industrial context, but the relationship between industrialism and urbanisation has proved never to be less than complicated. This is shown, for example, as soon as we try to establish boundaries of period. In demographic terms the first major period of urban expansion was in the second and third decades of the nineteenth century. But the historical process that we call, in so familiarly generalised terms, the 'Industrial Revolution', while notoriously difficult to define in terms of dates, was certainly well under way many years before the concentration of population within the cities that grew out of it. Furthermore, however we were to define our period, there were obvious dangers in talking of the cities as if they were a static entity: what might well be true of one point in time was hardly likely to hold good for another.

Industrialisation itself took very different forms in very different places. Just as not all cities in the nineteenth century were industrial, so not all industries found themselves situated in cities. For obvious symbolic reasons Manchester has come to be seen as archetypal, and as adoptive Mancunians we have found it difficult to resist its pre-eminence. But, strictly speaking, Manchester at the height of its powers was as much a commercial as an explicitly industrial city, acting as it did as a focal point for all those smaller north western towns – the 'Coketowns' of Dickens's *Hard Times* – in which the cotton industry was based. They, in English terms at least, are not cities at all – how often in this compilation we hankered for that American usage whereby any group of people living in close proximity can be defined as a city – but we could hardly exclude them from our consideration. Across the Pennines, in the case of the woollen industry, the situation was arguably more diverse, Bradford taking over from Leeds at about mid-century the pre-eminence which, where cotton was concerned, Manchester held from the start. Turning to the Midlands, and to Birmingham, we find a more varied pattern of industrial development creating its own kind of urban experience. Further difference is provided by, for example, Sheffield, Nottingham and Leicester ('towns', incidentally, or 'cities'?) with their expansion built upon single specialist industries, not to mention Liverpool, whose status, as compared, for example, with that of Bristol, was determined directly by industrial factors, but which can only awkwardly be defined as an industrial city in its own right.

Our approach to these problems has been, of necessity, pragmatic. The period chosen, 1820–1870, has allowed us to illustrate urban experience in industrial settings at a particularly significant stage in their development. By 1820 the towns and cities we have chosen to concentrate upon were firmly established: by 1870, it is fair to say, in general terms, that the first major phase of their development was complete. Increasingly conscious during the course of our research that our definition of an industrial city needed to be a flexible one, we have gone for the evidence where we could find it, drawing, we hope, the necessary distinctions of time and place, while all the time assuming the existence of common ground. We have concentrated upon the obviously major cities, while going beyond them as and where it seemed appropriate to do so.

We are inevitably conscious of significant omissions. We reasonably assumed that we would not be short of evidence, and that indeed proved to be the case, to the point where we could only include a fraction of what was available. Above all though, the commitment to interrelate historical and literary sources inevitably pointed our study in certain directions to the exclusion of others. The most obvious area in which history and literature come together is that of cultural history, and this is where we ultimately found ourselves concentrating our attention. On the other hand we offer very little on aspects of urban development which in a different context would come to the fore: on land-use, for example, on transportation, which we came to regard as a separate subject, and on what have come to be called the 'service industries', and specifically shopping, which we have had to neglect altogether.

Finally, we would want to insist upon a truth that has been increasingly borne in on us as we have worked on this project. The appeal to a multiplicity of sources is, on the face of it, an appeal to standards of objectivity. But a source can be read only in context; what it tells us is defined by the circumstances in which it is said. For the literary critic, interpretation of the text will depend upon its reference not only to external realities but to those texts which precede and surround it, as well as upon the formal conventions within which it operates. For the historian the perception of reality which documents convey will depend upon contexts not only of geographical location and historical moment, but of class and of gender. The 'contexts' and the 'commentary' which we offer have to be read with this continually in mind. And finally we should be conscious of all that unrecorded because unuttered history, of all that experience which failed to find its way into literary articulation. That is the most inescapable, and the most significant, omission of all.

DOROTHY SHELSTON
ALAN SHELSTON

1 A New Environment

Landscapes and Townscapes

In her novel *Felix Holt, the Radical* (1866), George Eliot took as her subject matter the condition of life in a Midlands community nearly forty years earlier. This choice of subject she was to amplify only a few years later in her next novel, *Middlemarch* (1871–2). Both novels were written in the shadow of the second Reform Bill of 1867; both concern themselves with changes inherent in those social movements which lay behind the first Reform Bill of 1832. In *Felix Holt* she announced her priorities in a carefully prepared 'Introduction', in which she takes her reader on an imaginary journey by stagecoach 'five and thirty years ago' through 'that central plain, watered at one extremity by the Avon, at the other by the Trent'. Referring to the possibility that transportation might become even more expeditious, she calls up an idealised memory of the old coaching days:

> Posterity may be shot, like a bullet from a tube, by atmospheric pressure from Winchester to Newcastle: that is a fine result to have among our hopes; but the slow old-fashioned way of getting from one end of our country to the other is the better thing to have in the memory.

> George Eliot, *Felix Holt* (1866), Introduction.

She goes on to describe how a traveller, conveyed by coach, would see as his day passed a landscape representing both old and new, and expressive of a society in a state of slow but irreversible change. At first he sees the traditional landscape of the rural world:

As the morning silvered the meadows with their long

line of bushy willows marking the watercourses, or
burnished the golden corn-ricks clustered over the
long roofs of some midland homestead, he saw the
full-uddered cows driven from the pasture to the early
milking.

Ibid.

Later on 'there were trim cheerful villages too, with a neat
or handsome parsonage and grey church set in the midst' but,
as the traveller moves into the Midland counties, he comes
for the first time to an industrial setting, and as George Eliot
describes this new landscape she offers a double comment.
The new and unpredictable industrial and urban society
embodies threats to traditional stabilities, but at the same
time the old can tolerate, even absorb, the new:

> But as the day wore on the scene would change: the
> land would begin to be blackened with coal-pits, the
> rattle of the handlooms to be heard in hamlets and
> villages . . . The breath of the manufacturing town,
> which made a cloudy day and a red gloom by night
> on the horizon, diffused itself over all the surrounding
> country, filling the air with eager unrest . . . Yet there
> were the grey steeples too, and the churchyards, with
> their grassy mounds and venerable headstones, sleeping
> in the sunlight; there were broad fields and homesteads,
> and fine old woods covering a rising ground, or
> stretching far by the roadside, allowing only peeps at
> the park and mansion which they shut in from the
> working-day world. In these midland districts the
> traveller passed rapidly from one phase of English life
> to another: after looking down on a village dingy with
> coal-dust, noisy with the shaking of looms, he might
> skirt a parish all of fields, high hedges, and deep-rutted
> lanes; after the coach had rattled over the pavement of
> a manufacturing town, the scene of riots and trades-
> union meetings, it would take him in another ten
> minutes into a rural region, where the neighbourhood
> of the town was only felt in the advantages of a near

market for corn, cheese, and hay, and where men with a considerable banking account were accustomed to say that "they never meddled with politics themselves." The busy scenes of the shuttle and wheel, of the roaring furnace, of the shaft and the pulley, seemed to make but crowded nests in the midst of the large-spaced, slow-moving life of homesteads and far-away cottages and oak-sheltered parks.

Ibid.

George Eliot's message is ultimately of the inextricable interrelatedness of this varied and changing society. Change is inevitable, and it is clear that we are at a significant historical moment in time, but her gradualist analysis allows her to see it as part of a wider historical process.

George Eliot's 'Introduction' to *Felix Holt* is in a tradition of English topographical writing that can be traced back to at least the beginning of the previous century: Daniel Defoe's *Tour Through the Whole Island of Great Britain* (1724–5) and William Cobbett's *Rural Rides* (1830) are classics of the genre. And the contrast between rural and urban, provincial and metropolitan, extends back beyond this tradition: we find it, for example, in the drama of not only the Restoration, but the Jacobean and Elizabethan periods. With the country has always been associated, on the one hand, peace, beauty, tradition, and on the other squalor, poverty and ignorance. The connotations of the town have always been those of energy, innovation, civilisation, but also those of noise, ugliness and materialism. The ambiguities inherent in such terms as 'pastoral' and 'provincial', 'urban' and 'urbane' subsume such values. But if the growth of industrialism through the eighteenth and nineteenth centuries and the consequent accumulation of the population in manufacturing towns and cities reinforced these contrasts it also gave them a new dimension. The industrial cities of Victorian England were different in kind from those which had gone before. They were the product of major economic restructuring and were dominated by industry and commerce. The process of urbanisation itself was a major change in the structure of British society which fundamentally altered the balance between town and country: the new cities involved those who lived and worked within them in a radically different way of life. To see how much this is so we can compare George Eliot's overview of what she presents as a typical English landscape with one described by the other great Victorian novelist, Charles Dickens. It is fair to say that while George Eliot's fictional stance is instinctively retrospective, that of Dickens is primarily immediate and contemporary. In *The Old Curiosity Shop* (1840–1), a novel written a decade after the period covered by *Felix Holt*, Dickens too describes a journey through the Midlands, this time undertaken by the heroine of his novel, Little Nell, and the grandfather she is required, through the circumstances of the plot, to protect. Here they pass on the road from Birmingham to Wolverhampton:

> In all their journeying, they had never longed so ardently, they had never so pined and wearied, for the freedom of pure air and open country, as now. No, not even on that memorable morning, when, deserting their own home, they abandoned themselves to the mercies of a strange world, and left all the dumb and senseless things they had known and loved, behind – not even then, had they so yearned for the fresh solitudes of wood, hillside, and field, as now; when the noise and dirt and vapour of the great manufacturing town, reeking with lean misery and hungry wretchedness, hemmed them in on every side, and seemed to shut out hope, and render escape impossible . . .
>
> A long suburb of red brick houses, – some with patches of garden-ground, where coal-dust and factory smoke darkened the shrinking leaves, and coarse rank flowers; and where the struggling vegetation sickened and sank under the hot breath of kiln and furnace, making them by its presence seem yet more blighting and unwholesome than the town itself, – a long, flat, straggling suburb passed, they came by slow degrees upon a cheerless region, where not a blade of grass was seen to grow; where not a bud put forth its

promise in the spring; where nothing green could live but on the surface of the stagnant pools, which here and there lay idly sweltering by the black roadside.

Advancing more and more into the shadow of this mournful place, its dark depressing influence stole upon their spirits, and filled them with a dismal gloom. On every side, and far as the eye could see into the heavy distance, tall chimneys, crowding on each other, and presenting that endless repetition of the same dull, ugly form, which is the horror of oppressive dreams, poured out their plague of smoke, obscured the light, and made foul the melancholy air. On mounds of ashes by the wayside, sheltered only by a few rough boards, or rotten pent-house roofs, strange engines spun and writhed like tortured creatures; clanking their iron chains, shrieking in their rapid whirl from time to time as though in torment unendurable, and making the ground tremble with their agonies. Dismantled houses here and there appeared, tottering to the earth, propped up by fragments of others that had fallen down, unroofed, windowless, blackened, desolate, but yet inhabited. Men, women, children, wan in their looks and ragged in attire, tended the engines, fed their tributary fires, begged upon the road, or scowled half-naked from the doorless houses. Then came more of the wrathful monsters, whose like they almost seemed to be in their wildness and their untamed air, screeching and turning round and round again; and still, before, behind, and to the right and left, was the same interminable perspective of brick towers, never ceasing in their black vomit, blasting all things living or inanimate, shutting out the face of day, and closing in on all these horrors with a dense dark cloud.

Charles Dickens, *The Old Curiosity Shop*
(1840–1), Ch. 45.

Dickens calls on the same basic contrast between rural and urban as George Eliot. Oppressed by the violence of the industrial scene, the child and her grandfather long for the 'freedom of pure air and open country', and the novel will eventually release them by bringing them to a Welsh border village far from the suffering endured during this phase of their journey. But where George Eliot qualifies the contrast and suggests the possibility of social integration, Dickens emphatically polarises it, suggesting only the inevitability of division. Furthermore the intensity of his account of the new urban world is such as to suggest that George Eliot's survey, sensitive though it is, is at best partial in its analysis of a changing society. There is little in her description of the Midlands landscape to suggest the overpowering impact of the new civilisation, little to suggest either its dynamism or its real cost. The difference, of course, can be at least partly explained by the experience that each of the novelists brought to the scenes they describe. George Eliot had grown up in the Midlands environment that she recalls, but significantly in the still provincial area of Coventry and Nuneaton, and not Birmingham, while Dickens writes as an outsider, recording what he sees with all the astonishment of someone who has never seen these things before.

Dickens's response to the industrial scene is one which is confirmed by many of his contemporaries, both from the world of London journalism and from abroad, who were seeing it for the first time. One of the most famous foreign commentators was Alexis de Tocqueville, who made two visits to England in the 1830s: he was never to write comprehensively about England as he did of the United States, but he recorded a number of impressions, amongst them this account of the physical appearance of Manchester which he visited in 1835:

> An undulating plain, or rather a collection of little hills. Below the hills a narrow river (the Irwell), which flows slowly to the Irish sea. Two streams (the Medlock and the Irk) wind through the uneven ground and after a thousand bends, flow into the river. Three canals made by man unite their tranquil, lazy waters at the same point. On this watery land, which nature and art have contributed to keep damp, are scattered

palaces and hovels. Everything in the exterior appearance of the city attests the individual powers of man; nothing the directing power of society. At every turn human liberty shows its capricious creative force. There is no trace of the slow continuous action of government.

Thirty or forty factories rise on the tops of the hills I have just described. Their six stories tower up; their huge enclosures give notice from afar of the centralisation of industry. The wretched dwellings of the poor are scattered haphazard around them. Round them stretches land uncultivated but without the charm of rustic nature, and still without the amenities of a town. The soil has been taken away, scratched and torn up in a thousand places, but it is not yet covered with the habitations of men. The land is given over to industry's use. The roads which connect the still-disjointed limbs of the great city, show, like the rest, every sign of hurried and unfinished work; the incidental activity of a population bent on gain, which seeks to amass gold so as to have everything else at once, and, in the intervals, mistrusts the niceties of life. Some of these roads are paved, but most of them are full of ruts and puddles into which foot or carriage wheel sinks deep. Heaps of dung, rubble from buildings, putrid, stagnant pools are found here and there among the houses and over the bumpy, pitted surfaces of the public places. No trace of surveyor's rod or spirit-level. Amid this noisome labyrinth from time to time one is astonished at the sight of fine stone buildings with Corinthian columns. It might be a medieval town with the marvels of the nineteenth century in the middle of it. But who could describe the interiors of those quarters set apart, home of vice and poverty, which surround the huge palaces of industry and clasp them in their hideous folds. On ground below the level of the river and overshadowed on every side by immense workshops, stretches marshy land which widely spaced muddy ditches can neither drain nor cleanse. Narrow, twisting roads lead down to it. They are lined with one-story houses whose ill-fitting planks and broken windows show them up, even from a distance, as the last refuge a man might find between poverty and death. None-the-less the wretched people reduced to living in them can still inspire jealousy of their fellow beings. Below some of their miserable dwellings is a row of cellars to which a sunken corridor leads. Twelve to fifteen human beings are crowded pell-mell into each of these damp, repulsive holes . . .

Look up and all around this place you will see the huge palaces of industry. You will hear the noise of furnaces, the whistle of steam. These vast structures keep light and air out of the human habitations which they dominate; they envelope them in perpetual fog; here is the slave, there the master; there the wealth of some, here the poverty of most; there the organised effort of thousands produce, to the profit of one man, what society has not yet learnt to give. Here the weakness of the individual seems more feeble and helpless even than in the middle of a wilderness; here the effects, there the causes.

A sort of black smoke covers the city. The sun seen through it is a disc without rays. Under this half-daylight 300,000 human beings are ceaselessly at work. A thousand noises disturb this damp, dark labyrinth, but they are not at all the ordinary sounds one hears in great cities . . .

From this foul drain the greatest stream of human industry flows out to fertilise the whole world. From this filthy sewer pure gold flows. Here humanity attains its most complete development and its most brutish; here civilisation works its miracles, and civilised man is turned back almost into a savage.

Alexis de Tocqueville, *Journeys to England and Ireland*, trans. G. Lawrence and K. P. Mayer, ed. J. P. Mayer (1958), pp. 105–8.

Manchester and Birmingham, as de Tocqueville himself pointed out, are very different cities, but here, just as in the
passage from *The Old Curiosity Shop*, we can see how the
process of industrialisation has transformed the landscape.
De Tocqueville observes the same details as Dickens: the
factories dominating the landscape, their smoke and noise
polluting the atmosphere, the haphazard development of sub-
human dwelling places, many of them in a state of collapse,
the complete destruction of the natural habitat. Even more
than Dickens, he dramatises the extremes, seeing them as
symbolic of a new pattern of human relationships, and
emphasising above all the consequences for this society of the
economic presuppositions on which it is based. It is interesting
to find de Tocqueville's observations on Manchester confirmed some twenty years later by a resident Manchester
novelist, Harrison Ainsworth who, in his autobiographical
novel *Mervyn Clitheroe*, wrote:

> What a wondrous town is Cottonborough
> [Manchester]! How vast – how populous – how ugly –
> how sombre! Full of toiling slaves, pallid from close
> confinement and heated air. Full of squalor, vice,
> misery: yet also full of wealth and all its concomitants –
> luxury, splendour, enjoyment. The city of coal and
> iron – the city of the factory and the forge – the city
> where greater fortunes are amassed, and more quickly,
> than in any other in the wide world. But how – and
> at what expense?
>
> William Harrison Ainsworth, *Mervyn Clitheroe*
> (1851–8), Ch. 8.

In the extracts by George Eliot, Dickens and de Tocqueville,
we see change as it is recorded by a traveller, a visitor to the
scene; the emphasis is on the transformation of the landscape.
Ainsworth, by contrast, was born in the city he describes.
His case reminds us that there is another perspective which
we must consider, and that is the way the cities themselves
changed as a consequence of industrial and economic development: we need to see the insider's as well as the outsider's

view. In the speed at which it developed Manchester was to some extent an unrepresentative city: cities like Sheffield and Birmingham, with their wealth founded upon the development of traditional industries rather than, as in Manchester's case, dramatic advances in technology, grew more gradually over the second half of the eighteenth and the first half of the nineteenth centuries. In another of her novels, *Silas Marner* (1861), George Eliot describes how the old hand-loom weaver returns at the end of his life to the town of his birth in search of the chapel where he had worshipped as a young man. He can find no trace of it: the yard where it had stood is dominated by a factory. The effect of this kind of change in the case of Birmingham is recorded in a broadside ballad attributed to James Dobbs, a music-hall performer, and native of the city. Dobbs died in 1837, so the poem must have been written rather before the journey described in *The Old Curiosity Shop*. It offers a more intimate response to changes in a known landscape and, while it opens by emphasising the writer's sense of disorientation, as it continues it develops a tone of cheerful acceptance and concludes indeed on a note of positive optimism.

> Full twenty years and more are passed,
> Since I left Brummagem,
> But I set out for home at last,
> To good old Brummagem,
> But ev'ry place is altered so,
> Now there's hardly a place I know,
> Which fills my heart with grief and woe,
> For I can't find Brummagem.
>
> As I was walking down our street,
> As used to be in Brummagem,
> I knowed nobody I did meet,
> For they've changed their face in Brummagem,
> Poor old Spiceal Street's half gone,
> And Old church stands alone,
> And poor old I stands here to groan,
> For I can't find Brummagem.

But amongst the changes we have got,
In good old Brummagem,
They've made a market on the moat,
To sell the pigs in Brummagem,
But that has brought us more ill luck
For they've filled up Pudding Brook,
Where in the brook jack-bannils [sticklebacks] took,
Near good old Brummagem.

But what's more melancholy still,
For poor old Brummagem,
They've taken away all Newhall-Hill
From poor old Brummagem,
At Easter time girls fair and brown,
Came rolly-polly down,
And showed their legs to half the town,
Oh! the good old sights of Brummagem.

Down Peck Lane I walked along,
To find out Brummagem,
There was the dungil down and gone
What no rogues in Brummagem,
They've ta'en it to a street called Moor,
A sign that rogues ain't fewer,
But rogues won't like it there I'm sure,
While Peck Lane's in Brummagem.

I remember one John Growse,
Who buckles made in Brummagem,
He built himself a country house,
To be out of the smoke of Brummagem,
But though John's country house stands still,
The town has walked up hill,
Now he lives beside a smoky mill,
In the middle of Brummagem.

Among the changes that abound,
In good old Brummagem,
May trade and happiness be found,
In good old Brummagem,

And tho' no Newhall Hill we've got,
Nor Pudding Brook nor Moat,
May we always have enough,
To boil the pot in Brummagem.

James Dobbs, 'I can't find Brummagem',
reprinted in *Victoria's Inferno*, ed. Jon Raven
(1978), pp.16–18.

Dobbs's ballad records a number of changes inherent in the development of the cities: the building of new streets in the city centres, the provision of new and enlarged institutional buildings – in this case the gaol – and the rapid encroachment of the city upon the surrounding countryside. It was written too early, however, to take in what was arguably the most significant single force for change where the industrial townscape was concerned – the coming of the railways. In a famous passage in *Dombey and Son* Dickens describes the building of the new Euston station:

The first shock of a great earthquake had, just at that period, rent the whole neighbourhood to its centre. Traces of its course were visible on every side. Houses were knocked down; streets broken through and stopped; deep pits and trenches dug in the ground; enormous heaps of earth and clay thrown up; buildings that were undermined and shaking, propped by great beams of wood. Here a chaos of carts, overthrown and jumbled together, lay topsy-turvy at the bottom of a steep unnatural hill; there confused treasures of iron soaked and rusted in something that had accidentally become a pond. Everywhere were bridges that led nowhere; thoroughfares that were wholly impassable; Babel towers of chimneys, wanting half their height; temporary wooden houses and enclosures, in the most unlikely situations; carcases of ragged tenements, and fragments of unfinished walls and arches, and piles of scaffolding, and wildernesses of bricks, and giant forms of cranes, and tripods straddling above nothing. There were a hundred thousand shapes and substances of incompleteness, wildly mingled out of their places, upside down, burrowing in the earth, aspiring in the air, mouldering in the water, and unintelligible as any dream. Hot springs and fiery eruptions, the usual attendants upon earthquakes, lent their contributions of confusion to the scene. Boiling water hissed and heaved within dilapidated walls; whence, also, the glare and roar of flames came issuing forth; and mounds of ashes blocked up rights of way, and wholly changed the law and custom of the neighbourhood.

In short, the yet unfinished and unopened Railroad was in progress; and from the very core of all this dire disorder, trailed smoothly away, upon its mighty course of civilisation and improvement.

Charles Dickens, *Dombey and Son* (1846–8), Ch. 6.

Similar scenes could have been observed in any of the major cities in the early and middle years of the Victorian period as the railway companies established their termini. What was crucial about this particular innovation was its wider effect, not only on the quality of life in the cities, but on their urban geography. As Lewis Mumford, the historian of the city, writes, 'Wherever the iron rails went, the mine and its debris went with them . . . The rushing locomotives brought noise, smoke, grit, into the hearts of the towns . . . the factories that grew up alongside the railway sidings mirrored the slatternly environment of the railroad itself.' (*The City in History*, Penguin edn 1966, p.513.) The development of the railway system is a subject of its own, and one well beyond the scope of this volume. Where the cities are concerned, however, it facilitated the commerce between them on which their expansion in many ways depended, while it transformed their physical appearance by the impact of its public buildings and works in ways that were not always, in Mumford's term, 'slatternly'. The great terminal stations gave new opportunities to architects eager to make their own contribution to the spirit of Victorian expansionism; the viaducts, tunnels and bridges which were often needed to bring the lines into the cities achieved a grandeur of their own. In 1829, on the eve of the railway age, Thomas Carlyle wrote in 'Signs of the Times', 'We remove mountains, and make seas our smooth highway; nothing can resist us. We war with rude Nature; and, by our resistless engines, come off always victorious, and loaded with spoils.' Carlyle was hardly an uncritical observer of his age, but his excitement here is genuine enough. If the industrial cities presented problems on a scale never before envisaged they equally embodied a potential for achievement on an heroic scale.

Demographic Trends

Nineteenth-century awareness that major changes were under way in British society was reinforced by evidence of a new type – that derived from official statistics. The decennial census held from 1801 onwards and the registration of births, deaths and marriages begun in England and Wales in 1837 meant that changes in the size and distribution of the population could be charted with increasing accuracy. Parliamentary reports drew heavily on this data in their analyses of social problems as can be seen in the following passage:

> By reference to the Population Returns it appears that, from the beginning of the present century, the whole population of Great Britain has increased at the rate of nearly 16 per cent every ten years; from 1801 to 1811, thence to 1821, and again to 1831; and there is every reason to believe about the same rate of increase will be found to have taken place next year, when the next decennial return will be made. Whilst, however, such has been the increase in the population of the kingdom at large, reference to the same returns shows that the augmentation of numbers in the great towns of the realm has been much more rapid: thus, whilst the increase of population in England and Wales, in thirty years, from 1801 to 1831, has been something more than 47 per cent, the actual increase in the

number of inhabitants of five of our most important
provincial towns has very nearly doubled that rate;
being:

Manchester	109 per cent
Glasgow	108 per cent
Birmingham	73 per cent
Leeds	99 per cent
Liverpool	100 per cent

giving an average of almost 98 per cent in five cities,
whose united population in 1831 amounted to 844,700,
and at the present time may be calculated at not less
than 1,126,000. Far the larger portion of this vast body
of persons are engaged constantly in occupations
connected with manufactures or commerce.

*Report of the Select Committee on the Health of
Large Towns and Populous Districts,
Parliamentary Papers* (1840) Vol. XI. p.279.

This passage identifies the two major demographic trends
of the nineteenth century, the overall growth of population
and its concentration in towns. The five great provincial cities
which on average doubled their populations between 1801
and 1831 repeated that process between 1831 and 1871.
Between 1801 and 1871 the population of Manchester grew
from 75 000 to 351 000, that of Glasgow from 77 000 to
478 000, Birmingham from 71 000 to 344 000, Leeds 53 000
to 259 000 and Liverpool 82 000 to 493 000 and the same
process was also underway in smaller towns and cities.

Adna Weber, the great pioneer in the study of urbanisation,
identifies the decade 1821–31 as the one in which the most
marked concentration of population in 'great cities' (those
with populations over 100 000) occurred. Almost all of these
cities were manufacturing towns in the north of England and
Weber concludes that 'It must therefore be clear to every
mind that the decade under discussion (1821–31) presents in
England a typical instance of the effect which the growth of
manufactures and the development of the factory system of
centralized industry has on the distribution of population.'
(*The Growth of Cities in the Nineteenth Century*, 1899,

p.53.) The decade 1841–51 saw the expansion of middle sized towns (20 000–100 000) which Weber sees as a consequence of the opening of the railways, particularly because of the effects this had on the growth of the iron industry, and the expansion of trade and commerce which accompanied the adoption of free trade. It was the ports and the iron producing and manufacturing towns which expanded most rapidly in these years.

For Weber the economic reorganisation which was part and parcel of the Industrial Revolution was responsible for this rapid urbanisation. In particular the greater opportunities for employment in the cities and the failure of rural employment to keep pace with population growth were major factors which gave rise to migration to the towns. Weber describes this migration as 'a "drift" towards the great centers by successive stages' (Ibid. p.258). It was not direct from field to city but rather short stage migration, into the city from the surrounding areas, gaps being filled by those from further afield. This process is described in relation to Glasgow in evidence quoted in the *Seventeenth Report on the Operation of the Poor Law Amendment Act* (1838):

> Taking Glasgow as the centre, there are persons who have come to it from all sides, within a circuit of sixty miles. My father originally came from the Lothians, and had been a country farmer; he was driven out by the improvements in farming, became a mechanic and settled in Glasgow. Most of my acquaintances either were born in the country or their parents came directly from the country. When the extinction of small farms took place, and the cottiers [sic] were driven in from their agricultural and pastoral employments, they first collected in villages, and then gradually inclined to the large towns, especially to Glasgow, from the Lothians. In my opinion, the population of Glasgow may be divided into five parts, of which the native inhabitants would be one-fifth, the Lowlanders two-fifths, the Highlanders one-fifth, and the Irish one-fifth.
>
> cit. A. Redford, *Labour Migration in England, 1800–1850* (1926), p.57.

Here it is suggested that it was the problems experienced by small farmers which led them to leave the land for the city. To them can be added the rural craftsmen who found they could not compete with cheap factory-produced goods distributed by railways. These were the 'push' factors which made it difficult for people to remain in the rural areas in which they were born. It is important however not to underestimate the 'pull' factors which attracted people to the towns and cities, for even in the period of agricultural prosperity in the third quarter of the century the flow of migrants from the rural areas continued. Except in years of very bad trade higher wages, greater variety of employment and more opportunities for advancement were all attractions of town life. Despite the overcrowding and poor living conditions the towns acted like magnets, drawing people in from the surrounding areas. Most migrants were young adults and for them the cities offered a new and different way of life. For women, despite the adverse sex imbalance, they offered a greater chance of marriage. Mrs Gaskell in *Mary Barton* describes her hero's wife as having,

> the fresh beauty of the agricultural districts; and somewhat of the deficiency of sense in her countenance which is likewise the characteristic of the rural inhabitants in comparison with the natives of the manufacturing towns.

> Elizabeth Gaskell, *Mary Barton* (1848), Ch. 1.

Another character in the same novel, an old woman, Alice Wilson, describes the way in which she had left rural north Lancashire years before to find work in Manchester. She is an example of this pattern of short stage migration, having stayed within the county of her birth but moved from its rural to its industrial region:

> 'Why, lass, there's nothing to tell. There was more mouths at home than could be fed. Tom, that's Will's father . . . had come to Manchester, and sent word that terrible lots of work was to be had, both for lads

and lasses. So father sent George first . . . and then work was scarce out towards Burton, where we lived, and father said I maun try get a place. And George wrote as how wages were far higher in Manchester than Milnethorpe or Lancaster; and, lasses, I was young and thoughtless, and thought it was a fine thing to go so far from home. So, one day, th' butcher he brings a letter fra George, to say he'd heard on a place – and I was all agog to go, and father was pleased like; but mother said little, and that little was very quiet. I've often thought she was a bit hurt to see me so ready to go – God forgive me! . . . She did not cry, though the tears was often in her eyes; and I seen her looking after me down the lane as long as I was in sight, with her hand shading her eyes – and that were the last look I ever had on her.

Mary Barton, Ch. 4.

Here we find both the 'push' factor, the shortage of work in the rural area, and the 'pull' factor, the high wages in Manchester and the excitement of travelling far from home, both of which contributed to the migration of the towns.

A major exception to this pattern of relatively short-stage migration was that of the Irish to the industrial towns of Britain. J. R. McCulloch in his *Account of the British Empire* (1854) drew attention to the significance of this migration to the industrial towns on the western side of the country and also to the anxieties to which it gave rise.

Within the last few years, however, an immigration has taken place into England, and also into Scotland, that has already had a great, and promises to have a still greater, influence over the blood and character of the people. We allude to the immigration of Irish, or Celtic, labourers into Great Britain. Considering the want of employment, and the low rate of wages in Ireland, the temptation to emigrate to England is all but irresistible; and steam communication has reduced the expenses of transit to almost nothing; having established, as it were, floating bridges between Dublin and Liverpool, Belfast and Glasgow, Waterford and Bristol. In consequence, very many thousands of Irish labourers have established themselves in Lancashire, Lanarkshire and other places, principally on the west coast of England and Scotland. So great indeed has been this immigration, that, at present, it is believed about a *fourth part* of the population of Manchester and Glasgow consists of native Irish and of the descendents of such; and in other places the proportion of Irish blood is even greater. Instead of being diminished, this influx, great as it has been, has latterly been augmented, and threatens to entail very pernicious consequences on the people of England and Scotland. The wages of the latter have been reduced by the competition of the Irish; and, which is still worse, their opinions in regard to what is necessary for their comfortable and decent subsistence have been lowered by the contaminating influence of example, and by familiar intercourse with those who are content to live in filth and misery. It is difficult to see how, with the existing facilities of intercourse between the two countries, the condition of the labouring classes in them should not be pretty much approximated; and there is too much reason to fear that the equalisation will be brought about rather by the degradation of the English than by the elevation of the Irish. Hitherto the latter have been very little, if at all, improved by their residence in England; but the English and Scots with whom they associate have been certainly deteriorated. Though painful and difficult, the importance of the subject gives it the strongest claims on the public attention. It were better that measures should be adopted to check, if that be possible, the spread of pauperism in Ireland, and to improve the condition of its inhabitants; but, if this cannot be done, it seems indispensable that we should endeavour to guard against being overrun by a pauper horde.

J. R. McCulloch, *Account of the British Empire*,
4th edn (1854), p.395.

McCulloch was writing after the Potato Famine had trig-
gered massive migration from Ireland which, together with
the deaths from starvation, resulted in the decrease in the
population of that country from 8.2 millions in 1841 to 6.5
millions in 1851. Writing before those terrible events Thomas
Carlyle expressed similar concern about Irish immigration.
The Irish had the reputation for being able to outwork and
underlive the British and the worst descriptions of living
conditions in the industrial towns relate to those districts
where they lived.

> Crowds of miserable Irish darken all our towns.
> The wild Milesian features, looking false ingenuity,
> restlessness, unreason, misery and mockery, salute you
> on all highways and byways. The English coachman, as
> he whirls past, lashes the Milesian with his whip,
> curses him with his tongue; the Milesian is holding
> out his hat to beg. He is the sorest evil this country
> has to strive with. In his rags and laughing savagery,
> he is there to undertake all work that can be done by
> mere strength of hand and back; for wages that
> will purchase him potatoes. He needs only salt for
> condiment; he lodges to his mind in any pighutch or
> doghutch, roosts in outhouses; and wears a suit of
> tatters, the getting off and on of which is said to be a
> difficult operation, transacted only in festivals and the
> hightides of the calendar. The Saxon man if he cannot
> work on these terms, finds no work. He too may be
> ignorant; but he has not sunk from decent manhood to
> squalid apehood; he cannot continue there. American
> forests lie untilled across the ocean; the uncivilised
> Irishman, not by his strength, but by the opposite of
> strength, drives out the Saxon native, takes possession
> in his room. There abides he, in his squalor and
> unreason, in his falsity and drunken violence, as the
> ready made nucleus of degradation and disorder.

Thomas Carlyle, *Chartism* (1840), Ch. 4.

Migration was not the only factor which added to the

numbers living in the cities; they also grew by natural increase, the excess of births over deaths. This was in part a product of migration in that the people who came to the towns were mainly young adults, of an age to get married and have children. Marriage rates were higher in the towns and age at marriage lower, both factors which encouraged high fertility. The outcome was a birth-rate high enough to exceed even the high death-rate produced by unhealthy living conditions. This is apparent from Edwin Chadwick's *Report on the Sanitary Condition of the Labouring Population of Great Britain* presented to Parliament in 1842. Chadwick used the great wealth of statistical data which had become available to demonstrate the links between poor living conditions, ill health and high mortality; the economic and social costs of ill health and bad housing; and the need to set up an administrative framework capable of handling these problems. His statistics show that natural increase was occurring in all the counties of England. Included in the counties with the highest mortality are the industrial counties with rapidly expanding towns – Lancashire, the West Riding of Yorkshire, Northumberland, Durham and the Midland counties of Nottinghamshire, Leicestershire and Worcestershire. But in every case the number of births exceeds the number of deaths and, taken as a group, the counties with the highest death rate also have the highest birth rate.

> By means of the last census and the last year's completed registration of deaths and births in England, I am enabled to show that there has been an increase of the population from births alone in those parts of the country where the proportionate mortality is the greatest.
> Taking the 42 counties as I find them arranged in Mr. Porter's paper on the census; dividing them into three parts, viz., the 14 counties where there has been the least proportionate mortality, the 14 counties where the proportion of mortality has been the greatest, and the 14 counties where the proportion of mortality has been intermediate, I find the results as to the

proportionate increase of births to the increase of deaths to be as follows:

	The annual average Rate of Increase of Population has been per 10,000 persons between 1831 and 1841	Proportion of Births and Deaths to Population in the Year ended June 30, 1840	Proportion of Births and Deaths to every 10,000 Persons in same period	Excess in every 10,000 Persons of Births above Deaths
a. The 14 counties where the mortality has been *the least*	112	deaths (1 in 54), births (1 in 34),	deaths 184 births 297	113
b. The 14 counties where it has been *intermediate*	121	deaths (1 in 48), births (1 in 33).	deaths 208 births 302	94
c. The 14 counties where it has been the greatest	183	deaths (1 in 39), births (1 in 29),	deaths 259 births 348	89

Edwin Chadwick, *Report on the Sanitary Condition of the Labouring Population of Great Britain* (1842), ed. M. W. Flinn (1965), p.248.

In Chadwick's work, in the investigations of the local statistical societies and, after its formation in 1857, in the papers presented to the National Association for the Promotion of Social Science we find great emphasis placed on the collection and analysis of statistical data. Not everyone shared this enthusiasm. Writers like Carlyle and Dickens, resolutely opposed to the utilitarian priority of 'Fact', insisted that statistics ignore those things which cannot be measured. 'With what serene conclusiveness a member of some Useful-Knowledge Society stops your mouth with a figure of arithmetic!' Carlyle exclaimed in *Chartism*. But such attitudes are caught up in paradox, since it was statistical enquiry which provided the basis for the reforms that these writers demanded.

Social Patterns

Writing in 1840, William Cooke Taylor, an Irish journalist and traveller, described the northern cities as 'a system of social life constructed on a wholly new principle, a principle yet vague and indefinite but developing itself by its own spontaneous force and daily producing effects which no human foresight had predicted.' (cit. E. Lampard, 'The Urbanising World', in H. J. Dyos and Michael Wolff, (eds), *The Victorian City: Images and Realities*, Vol. I, p.5). This conception of the industrial city as a new kind of social organism which generated its own patterns of social relationships is to be found in the writings of many nineteenth- and twentieth-century commentators. Contrasts are frequently made between the traditional small scale rural community based on close personal relationships and modern, large scale, complicated urban society where relationships are impersonal and transitory. The urban sociologist Ferdinand Tonnies, for example, writing in 1887, distinguishes between 'Gemeinschaft' (community), a social order based on close personal relationships, with a sense of community which comes from being brought up in a particular locality among family and friends, and 'Gesellschaft' (association), the superficial, self-interested relationships which are the characteristic of industrial society.

The experience of loss involved in moving from the country to the town is explored in two sonnets by Hartley Coleridge written in Leeds in 1832. Separation from a known landscape together with the loss of a sense of personal identity which comes from knowing people and being known by them are dimensions of this process which induces an intense feeling of personal isolation.

(i)
I left the land where men with Nature dwelling,
Know not how much they love her lovely forms –
Nor heed the history of forgotten storms,
On the blank folds inscribed of drear Helvellyn;
I sought the town, where toiling, buying, selling –
Getting and spending, poising hope and fear,

Make but one season of the live-long year.
Now for the brook from moss-girt fountain welling,
I see the foul stream hot with sleepless trade;
For the slow creeping vapours of the morn,
Black hurrying smoke, in opaque mass up-borne.
O'er dinning engines hangs, a stifling shade –
Yet Nature lives e'en here, and will not part
From her best home, the lowly loving heart.

(ii)
'Tis strange to me, how long have seen no face,
That was not like a book, whose every page
I knew by heart, a kindly common-place,
And faithful record of progressive age –
To wander forth, and view an unknown race;
Of all that I have been, to find no trace,
No footstep of my by-gone pilgrimage.
Thousands I pass, and no one stays his pace
To tell me that the day is fair or rainy;
Each one his object seeks with anxious chase,
And I have not a common hope with any;
Thus like one drop of oil upon a flood,
In uncommunicating solitude,
Single am I amid the countless many.

> Hartley Coleridge, *Complete Poetical Works*, ed.
> Ramsay Colles (1908), p.15.

The focus here is on the individual's awareness of change
and its consequences, but of greater concern for many
observers were the social consequences of urban concentration, and in particular concern about the maintenance of
social control in cities and towns dominated by a rapidly
multiplying working class. The *Report of the Select Committee
on the Health of Large Towns* from which we have already
quoted (see pp.14–15), for example, suggests that,

> It must be evident, that owing to this rapid increase
> in the population of great towns, the proportion of
> the humbler classes, of those with little leisure for
> education or improvement, will be augmented, as

the more wealthy and educated gradually withdraw themselves from these close and crowded communities; thus more and more stand in need of some superintending paternal care.

op. cit., p.280.

Cooke Taylor expresses this anxiety far more forcibly in his *Notes of a Tour in the Manufacturing Districts of Lancashire*, 1842.

It would be absurd to speak of Factories as mere abstractions, and consider them apart from the manufacturing population – that population is a stern reality, and cannot be neglected with impunity. As a stranger passes through the masses of human beings which have been accumulated round the mills and print works in this and the neighbouring towns, he cannot contemplate these 'crowded hives' without feelings of anxiety and apprehension almost amounting to dismay. The population, like the system to which it belongs, is NEW; but it is hourly increasing in breadth and strength. It is an aggregate of masses, our conceptions of which clothe themselves in terms that express something portentous and fearful. We speak not of them indeed as of sudden convulsions, but as of the slow rising and gradual swelling of an ocean, which must, at some future and no distant time, bear all the elements of society aloft upon its bosom, and float them – Heaven knows whither. There are mighty energies slumbering in those masses: had our ancestors witnessed the assemblage of such a multitude as is poured forth every evening from the mills of Union Street, magistrates would have assembled, special constables would have been sworn, the riot act read, the military called out, and most probably some fatal collision would have taken place. The crowd now scarcely attracts the notice of a passing policeman, but it is, nevertheless, a crowd, and therefore susceptible of the passions which may animate a multitude.

The most striking phenomenon of the Factory system is the amount of population which it has suddenly accumulated on certain points: there has been long a continuous influx of operatives into the manufacturing districts from other parts of Britain; these men have very speedily laid aside all their old habits and associations, to assume those of the mass in which they are mingled. The manufacturing population is not new in its formation alone: it is new in its habits of thought and action, which have been formed by the circumstances of its condition, with little instruction, and less guidance, from external sources. It may be matter of question whether the circumstances surrounding the manufacturing labourer are better or worse than those belonging to the agricultural condition, but there can be no doubt that the former are preferred by the operative. In the present severe pressure of commercial distress there are scores, and probably hundreds, of workmen, whom the authorities would gladly send back to their parishes if they could bring them legally under the designation of paupers, but these men submit to the pressure of hunger, and all its attendant sufferings, with an iron endurance which nothing can bend, rather than be carried back to an agricultural district. However severe the condition of the manufacturing operative may be, there is something behind which he dreads more: he clings to his new state with desperate fidelity, and faces famine rather than return to the farm. The Factory system is, therefore, preferred to the more usual conditions of labour by the population which it employs, and this at once ensures its permanence as a formative element of society, and at the same time renders its influence directly efficacious on character.

I have visited Manchester at seasons when trade was pre-eminently prosperous: I see it now suffering under severe and unprecedented distress; and I have been very forcibly struck by observing the little change which the altered circumstances have produced in the moral aspect of the population. Agricultural distress soon makes itself known; Swing at this side of the water, and Rock at the other, write the tales of their grievances in characters which no man can mistake, and seek redress by measures strongly marked with the insanity of despair. But suffering here has not loosened the bands of confidence; millions of property remain at the mercy of a rusty nail or the ashes of a tobacco-pipe, and yet no one feels alarm for the safety of his stock or machinery, though in case of an operative *Jacquerie* they could not be defended by all the military force of England. This very crisis has been a rigid test of the strength of the Factory system, and precludes the necessity of any further argument to show that it cannot be overthrown.

W. Cooke Taylor, Notes of a Tour in the
Manufacturing Districts of Lancashire (1842), pp.6–9.

Cooke Taylor insists that the manufacturing towns are 'NEW', a phenomenon different in kind from anything that has gone before; his observation of a large orderly population going about its daily business arouses in him 'anxiety and apprehension amounting almost to dismay'. Not because he fears riots and attacks on property – the urban population is favourably contrasted with the rural population in this respect – but because he fears the power of numbers and the breakdown of the existing pattern of class dominance. He is struck by the commitment of the urban workers to their new situation: at a time of severe depression they are prepared to starve rather than ask for help from the Poor Law and so risk being sent back to their rural parishes. He sees the possibility that the urban working class could develop its own identity, adopting ways of thinking and behaving which are not shaped by the ruling classes but are an independent response to their own situation.

Cooke Taylor's anxieties were provoked by his observation of Manchester. Manchester is also the example that Friedrich Engels uses to illustrate the new organising principle on which he believes the manufacturing cities are based, that of the segregation and polarisation of classes.

Owing to the curious lay-out of the town it is quite possible for someone to live for years in Manchester and to travel daily to and from his work without ever seeing a working-class quarter or coming into contact with an artisan. He who visits Manchester simply on business or for pleasure need never see the slums, mainly because the working-class districts and the middle-class districts are quite distinct. This division is due partly to deliberate policy and partly to instinctive and tacit agreement between the two social groups . . . In the centre of Manchester there is a fairly large commercial district, which is about half a mile long and half a mile broad. This district is almost entirely given over to offices and warehouses. Nearly the whole of this district has no permanent residents and is deserted at night, when only policemen patrol its dark, narrow thoroughfares with their bull's eye lanterns. This district is intersected by certain main streets which carry an enormous volume of traffic. The lower floors of the buildings are occupied by shops of dazzling splendour. A few of the upper stories on these premises are used as dwellings and the streets present a relatively busy appearance until late in the evening. Around this commercial quarter there is a belt of built up areas on the average one and a half miles in width, which is occupied entirely by working-class dwellings. This area of workers' houses includes all Manchester proper, except the centre, all Salford and Hulme, and important parts of Pendleton and Chorlton, two-thirds of Ardwick and certain small areas of Cheetham Hill and Broughton. Beyond this belt of working-class houses or dwellings lie the districts inhabited by the middle classes and the upper classes. The former are to be found in regularly laid out streets near the working-class districts – in Chorlton and in the remoter parts of Cheetham Hill. The villas of the upper classes are surrounded by gardens and lie in the higher and remoter parts of Chorlton and Ardwick or on the breezy heights of Cheetham Hill, Broughton and Pendleton. The upper classes enjoy healthy country air and live in luxurious and comfortable dwellings which are linked to the centre of Manchester by omnibuses which run every fifteen or thirty minutes. To such an extent has the convenience of the rich been considered in the planning of Manchester that these plutocrats can travels from their houses to their places of business in the centre of the town by the shortest routes, which run entirely through working-class districts, without even realising how close they are to the misery and filth which lie on both sides of the road. This is because the main streets which run from the Exchange in all directions out of the town are occupied almost uninterruptedly on both sides by shops, which are kept by members of the lower middle classes. In their own interests these shopkeepers should keep the outsides of their shops in a clean and respectable condition, and in fact they do so ... Even the less pretentious shops adequately serve their purpose of hiding from the eyes of wealthy ladies and gentlemen with strong stomachs and weak nerves the misery and squalor which are part and parcel of their own riches and luxury ...

I am quite aware of the fact that this hypocritical town-planning device is more or less common to all big cities. I realise, too, that owing to the nature of their business, shopkeepers inevitably seek premises in main thoroughfares. I know that in such streets there are more good houses than bad ones, and that the value of the land is higher on or near a main thoroughfare than in the back streets. But in my opinion Manchester is unique in the systematic way in which the working classes have been barred from the main streets. Nowhere else has such care been taken to avoid offending the tender susceptibilities of the eyes and the nerves of the middle classes. Yet Manchester is the very town in which building has taken place in a haphazard manner with little or no planning or interference from the authorities. When the middle classes zealously proclaim that all is well with the working classes, I cannot help feeling that the politically 'progressive' industrialists, the Manchester 'bigwigs', are not quite so innocent of this shameful piece of town planning as they pretend.

> F. Engels, *The Condition of the Working Class in England* (1845) trans. and ed. W. O. Henderson and W. H. Chaloner (1958), pp.54–6.

Engels anticipates the urban sociologist of the Chicago School, Ernest Burgess, in his description of the city as a series of concentric circles occupied by different social groups around a commercial centre. The same criticisms have been made of both, that this pattern is an oversimplification and is not always borne out by empirical studies. But what comes through most strongly from this passage is Engels' perception of the way in which class division underpins urban life. Residential segregation is class-based and the polarisation of classes is demonstrated by the way in which the middle class are spared even the sight of the misery and squalor of working-class living conditions as they travel from the leafy suburbs to the commercial heart of the city. For Engels it is not the city itself which produces these patterns of class segregation and polarisation; they are the product of the capitalist economic infrastructure. But it is within the industrial cities that the conflicts within the capitalist system and the exploitation that it generates are most clearly demonstrated.

> What is true of London, is true also of all the great towns, such as Manchester, Birmingham and Leeds. Everywhere one finds on the one hand the most barbarous indifference and selfish egotism and on the other the most distressing scenes of misery and poverty. Signs of social conflict are to be found everywhere. Everyone turns his house into a fortress to defend himself – under the protection of the law – from the depredations of his neighbours. Class warfare is so open and shameless that it has to be seen to be believed. The observer of such an appalling state of affairs must shudder at the consequences of such feverish activity and can only marvel that so crazy a

social and economic structure should survive at all.

Engels, op. cit., p.31.

The sources we have quoted in this chapter are in different ways and to different degrees critical of the social environment created by the new industrialism. Although Engels, as does de Tocqueville in his account of this new society, notes salient differences between the cities he observes, as with other contemporary commentators his emphasis is on what he assumes to be the common features of urban life. A modern commentator, Richard Dennis, sees the predominantly negative tone of much contemporary comment as the outcome of 'the obsessions of the age, the political and cultural prejudices of observers, the expectations of their readers, as much as any "objective reality".' (*English Industrial Cities of the Nineteenth Century*, 1984, p.23.) Much of the commentary was written by middle-class men for a largely middle-class readership with little or no experience of the world that was being described. It was also an immediate response to a rapidly changing situation: the growth of the manufacturing towns may have produced temporary social dislocation rather than a permanent change in the pattern of human relationships. Communities did grow up within the urban environment; the sense of alienation felt by commentators from Wordsworth to T. S. Eliot and beyond can be at least partly attributed to their own cultural conditioning. A modern historian of the city, H. J. Dyos, has argued that, far from intensifying class division, 'the Victorian city was essentially a great leveller.' (*Exploring the Urban Past*, 1982, p.7.) But both the force of contemporary comment and the central focus of its analysis testify to the great contrast which was perceived between the rural and the urban way of life, and above all to the extremes to be found within the cities themselves: critical detachment was a facility available only to a later generation.

2 Living Conditions

The Dominance of Work

The factor which above all dictated the condition of life in the towns and cities of industrial Britain in the nineteenth century was their domination purely and simply by the demands of business and of work. The biblical text 'In the sweat of thy face shalt thou eat bread' acquired a new dimension in these industrial communities; owner and operative alike lived their lives in an environment which reflected the inescapable need to produce and to earn. New technologies, underpinned by the structures of capitalist economics, created new rigidities and re-defined the relationships between employers and employed. New disciplines of work evolved as time literally became money: the working day came to be measured not by the tasks to be fulfilled, but by the hours to be served. These new conditions were reflected in the disposition of housing for all classes, and thus in the physical development of the towns and cities themselves. As we shall see, different situations created different conditions, and here, as always in our consideration of the Victorian cities, we need to keep firmly in mind the particular characteristics of individual localities. But, whatever the individual circumstances, the dominance of work remains a constant within the urban environment, controlling the lives of, as the Prayer Book has it, 'all sorts and conditions of men'.

A graphic account of the way in which individual lives were conditioned by the demands of work is given in a working-class autobiography by 'An Old Potter' which first appeared as a series of articles in *The Staffordshire Sentinel* in the last decade of the nineteenth century. 'An Old Potter' was the pseudonym of Charles Shaw, a Methodist minister who was born in 1832 and who spent the early years of his life working in the Potteries. Here he describes his childhood experience:

I have said there was generally little, if any, work done on Mondays and Tuesdays, and yet it was rare for any of the men to get on Saturday less than a full week's wage. From Wednesday to Saturday they worked themselves, and worked others, like galley slaves. From four and five in the morning until nine and ten at night this fierce race for wages was run. There was no Factory Act then, nor for a quarter of a century afterwards. Women and children were then given up to the greed of employers, and to the drunken greed of many of their operative 'masters', as they were called. Many a time, after fourteen and fifteen hours' work, I had to walk a mile and a half home with another weary little wretch, and we have nodded and budged against each other on the road, surprised to find our whereabouts. No wonder ghosts were seen in the dark, gasless 'Hollow', with flashing lights of furnaces in the distance, and with noise of water from the flour mill in the valley. Oh, yes, I have seen ghosts and heard their wailings on such nights, when my senses were dazed with weariness. Boys don't see them now, even in the 'Hollow', because the Factory Act sends them home at six o'clock, and because the road is lit up with gas lamps. These long hours were worked too, on the poorest and most meagre fare. Bread and butter were made up in a handkerchief, with a sprinkling of tea and sugar. Sometimes there was a little potato pie, with a few pieces of fat bacon on it to represent beef. The dinner time was from one till two o'clock, and from then until nine or ten the weary workers got no more food. Weary for sleep, weak with hunger, and worn out with hard work, many wretched children, through summer and winter nights, had to make their way home at these late hours. Summer was no summer for them, except for warmth and light; while winter, dark and pitiless, always brought its full burden of horror and suffering.

'An Old Potter', *When I was a Child* (1903, reprinted 1977) pp.54–5.

The situation described here is one peculiar to the local industry. In that the potteries were not mechanised, the workers were free to absent themselves in the earlier part of the week: it was only as the week developed that they felt the pressure to achieve the required output. Later, Shaw was to be involved in the cotton industry, an experience that led him to reflect that if, in the Potteries, 'there had been a governing power like machinery, and if a steam-engine had started every Monday morning at six o'clock, the workers would have been disciplined to the habits of regular and continuous industry' (p.186). The benefit is one which later commentators in their turn have queried. But what is clear from the passage is the consequence of the 'fierce race for wages' on those – in this case the women and children – least able to defend themselves, and the way in which within the industry itself power structures evolved which perpetuated the worst aspects of the system. The 'operative "masters"' are themselves both controlled by the drive for production and forced by its demands to impose them on those beneath them. For the weakest of all there is scarcely any part of their waking life that is free from toil.

Given the dominance of work, and in particular the length of the working day, it was expedient that the work force should live as near as possible to their labour. For the young Charles Shaw the mile and a half he had to walk back to his home was clearly the final straw. At a much later point in time, Lady Bell, describing Middlesbrough, a city which in simple statistical terms provided the most striking example of urban growth in the nineteenth century, as 'a place in which every sense is violently assailed all day by some manifestation of the making of iron', nevertheless reflected on the advantage to the workers of living close to the foundries:

> From the point of view of the workmen there are even advantages in living in the centre of the works in these desolate surroundings; it means that instead of having a cold windy walk to and from their work every day they are on the spot. For it must be a substantial addition to the hardships of life to have every morning

and every night in the winter to cross that cold wind-
swept river with the additional walk on either side. It
is counted a privilege, therefore, to live in this strange
wild settlement, and since the number of cottages is
limited, it means that the workmen who live there
have a claim of some personal nature, usually that of
a long term of service.

Lady Bell, *At the Works* (1907), p.16.

Writing at the beginning of the twentieth century, Lady Bell
is looking back on a situation initiated by the discovery of
workable ironstone in the immediate vicinity in 1850, the
result of which was effectively a new industry leading to the
building of communities of closely packed houses. In the
Midlands, as in the Potteries, the evolution of industry at an
earlier stage through the multiplication of small family-based
concerns had resulted in a much more piecemeal pattern of
development. In Benjamin Disraeli's novel *Sybil*, set in the
same Midlands region as that described by Dickens in *The
Old Curiosity Shop*, (see pp.4–5) he depicts the township of
'Wodgate', a fictionalised version of Willenhall, Staffordshire:

Wodgate had the appearance of a vast squalid suburb.
As you advanced, leaving behind you long lines of
little dingy tenements, with infants lying about the
road, you expected every moment to emerge into
some streets, and encounter buildings bearing some
correspondence in their size and comfort to the considerable population swarming and busied around you.
Nothing of the kind. There were no public buildings
of any sort; no churches, chapels, town-hall, institute,
theatre; and the principal streets in the heart of the
town in which were situate the coarse and grimy shops,
though formed by houses of a greater elevation than
the preceding, were equally narrow and if possible
more dirty. At every fourth or fifth house, alleys
seldom above a yard wide, and streaming with filth,
opened out of the street. These were crowded with
dwellings of various size, while from the principal

court often branched out a number of smaller alleys, or rather narrow passages, than which nothing can be conceived more close and squalid and obscure. Here, during the days of business, the sound of the hammer and the file never ceased.

Benjamin Disraeli, *Sybil* (1845), Bk iii, Ch. 4.

We can usefully compare 'Wodgate' with Dickens's account of 'Coketown' in *Hard Times*:

It was a town of red brick, or of brick that would have been red if the smoke and ashes had allowed it; but as matters stood it was a town of unnatural red and black like the painted face of a savage. It was a town of machinery and tall chimneys, out of which interminable serpents of smoke trailed themselves for ever and ever, and never got uncoiled. It had a black canal in it, and a river that ran purple with evil-smelling dye, and vast piles of buildings full of windows where there was a rattling and a trembling all day long, and where the piston of the steam-engine worked monotonously up and down like the head of an elephant in a state of melancholy madness. It contained several large streets all very like one another, and many small streets still more like one another, inhabited by people equally like one another, who all went in and out at the same hours, with the same sound upon the same pavements, to do the same work, and to whom every day was the same as yesterday and to-morrow, and every year the counterpart of the last and the next.

These attributes of Coketown were in the main inseparable from the work by which it was sustained; against them were to be set off, comforts of life which found their way all over the world, and elegancies of life which made, we will not ask how much of the fine lady, who could scarcely bear to hear the place mentioned. The rest of its features were voluntary, and they were these.

You saw nothing in Coketown but what was severely workful. If the members of a religious persuasion built a chapel there – as the members of eighteen religious persuasions had done – they made it a pious warehouse of red brick, with sometimes (but this is only in highly ornamented examples) a bell in a birdcage on the top of it. The solitary exception was the New Church; a stuccoed edifice with a square steeple over the door, terminating in four short pinnacles like florid wooden legs. All the public inscriptions in the town were painted alike, in severe characters of black and white. The jail might have been the infirmary, the infirmary might have been the jail, the town-hall might have been either, or both, or anything else, for anything that appeared to the contrary in the graces of their construction. Fact, fact, fact, everywhere in the material aspect of the town; fact, fact, fact, everywhere in the immaterial. The M'Choakumchild school was all fact, and the school of design was all fact, and the relations between master and man were all fact, and everything was fact between the lying-in hospital and the cemetery, and what you couldn't state in figures, or show to be purchaseable in the cheapest market and saleable in the dearest, was not, and never should be, world without end, Amen.

Charles Dickens, *Hard Times* (1854), Bk I, Ch. 5.

Hard Times is the most famous of the Victorian industrial novels and 'Coketown' has come to be seen as symbolic of a new urban and industrial society: as Lewis Mumford has written, 'In a greater or lesser degree, every city in the Western World was stamped with the archetypal characteristics of Coketown.' (*The City in History*, 1961; Pelican edn, 1966, p.509) But if, like Disraeli's 'Wodgate', and indeed the accounts of the industrial landscape recorded in Chapter 1, 'Coketown' is completely dominated by its industry, there are important differences. In Disraeli's account development is entirely haphazard, and it excludes anything not immediately connected with the processes of production. 'Coketown', by comparison, is the epitome of order and system, while its development has included the churches, the town hall and the other public buildings – a 'library' for example, 'to which general access was easy' (Bk I, Ch. 8) – which 'Wodgate' expressly lacks. The differences are between kinds of industry and the kinds of community they created. 'Coketown' is a fictional construct, and not a real place, but for all its symbolic significance it reflected a particular kind of urban experience which was confirmed by Dickens's visit in 1854 to the Lancashire town of Preston, where he had gone to observe industrial conditions almost immediately after starting work on his novel. Whereas the industries of the Midlands, on which Disraeli based his observations in *Sybil*, were based on small units of considerable diversity, the rapidly growing cotton-towns of the North of England were single industry communities, organised around large factories using mechanical power and employing a substantial labour force. It is in this situation that the remorseless conformities of time-keeping, of repetitive labour, of living conditions and of civic life take on their symbolic weight, but we should not necessarily see the situation itself as typical. What Disraeli and Dickens both insist upon, however, is the way in which industry itself determines every aspect of life within the urban community.

What lies at the core of Dickens's account of 'Coketown', of course, is his unshakeable opposition to the utilitarian ethic, of which he saw it as the ultimate physical manifestation. His visit to Preston was undertaken not so much in a spirit of enquiry as in confirmation of an already determined position, and it is interesting that nowhere in *Hard Times* does he reveal the mixed response that he shows elsewhere in his novels towards the power and energy embodied in the Victorian achievement. For him the all-pervading social ethic is seen entirely in negative terms. But, as we have seen, 'Coketown' does have its churches and public buildings: its opening chapter is famously set in a school founded by the local eminence, Thomas Gradgrind, who ensures that the teaching will be conducted on soundly functionalist lines. As Dennis points out, 'To the early Victorian middle classes there was no question that their poor ought not to be left alone.' (*English Industrial Cities of the Nineteenth Century* (1984), p.52).

When we come to consider the great cities we come up against a much more complicated situation. In the first place the cities themselves were much more complex organisms than the factory towns. None of them was entirely of nineteenth-century creation, and they all embodied a multiplicity of functions. Manchester itself, the capital of the cotton industry, and Leeds, the equivalent centre of the woollen trade, for example, inevitably developed substantial and complex commercial infrastructures that diversified the pattern of social relationships as the century developed. The same was true of Birmingham, while the great seaports like Liverpool and Bristol were established on entirely different foundations.

Within the manufacturing cities it remained possible to conceive of situations where master and men lived in close contiguity well on into the nineteenth century. In *North and South*, Mrs Gaskell's second Manchester novel, the industrialist, Mr Thornton, is depicted as living within his own factory yard:

> The lodge-door was like a common garden-door; on one side of it were great closed gates for the ingress and egress of lorries and wagons. The lodge-keeper admitted them into a great oblong yard, on one side of which were offices for the transaction of business; on the opposite, an immense many-windowed mill, whence proceeded the continual clank of machinery and the long groaning roar of the steam-engine, enough to deafen those who lived within the enclosure. Opposite to the wall, along which the street ran, on one of the narrow sides of the oblong, was a handsome stone-coped house – blackened, to be sure, by the smoke, but with paint, windows, and steps kept scrupulously clean. It was evidently a house which had been built some fifty or sixty years. The stone facings – the long, narrow windows and the number of them – the flights of steps up to the front door, ascending from either side, and guarded by railing – all witnessed to its age. Margaret only wondered why people who could afford to live in so good a house, and keep it in such perfect order, did not prefer a

much smaller dwelling in the country, or even some
suburb; not in the continual whirl and din of the
factory.

Elizabeth Gaskell, *North and South* (1855), Ch. 15.

The heroine's query is a valid one since, as we have seen
from Engels's account of Manchester ten years earlier, Mr
Thornton's preference is somewhat unusual by this date. A
House of Lords committee of 1842 was told that in Birmingham, 'The more opulent inhabitants reside in the surrounding country: comparatively few live in the town', while
within the towns themselves 'the better houses are generally
inhabited by master manufacturers, or the superintendents of
their concerns to whom it is convenient and advantageous to
live near their works.' (cit. Dennis, op. cit., p.55). 'Near',
that is, but not 'in'. *North and South*, if usually regarded as
a Manchester novel, is in fact more fictional in its invention
of locations than the earlier *Mary Barton* where, in confirmation of Engels, master and men live in different parts of
the city, and where Mrs Gaskell makes a specific point of
emphasising the distance, physical and symbolic, between
them. In the 'Preface' to *Mary Barton* Mrs Gaskell writes that
she 'bethought how deep might be the romance in the lives
of some of those who elbowed me daily in the busy streets
of the town in which I resided.' The irony is that while the
city and its streets provided a context for the interaction of
different social classes the divisions it was beginning to
embody meant that they knew little of each other's lives.

As the industrial cities grew, and their populations
increased, so the divisions between those who lived and
worked in them were reinforced. Residential areas became
differentiated by class and by status, the rich gathering in the
more exclusive enclaves while the poorest districts effectively
became ghettoes for the most vulnerable sections of the
working class. On the perimeters of the cities new suburbs
were built to accommodate the increasing numbers of workers
whose employment was not itself industrial, but was a
consequence of industrial progress – the clerks, small managers
and commercial employees, predecessors of Mr Pooter – who

were amongst the first commuters. The development of
suburban railways as early as the 1840s and 50s led to the
building of further and more prestigious suburbs at a greater
distance – in the case of Manchester, for example, at Alderley
Edge, Altrincham and Bowdon. All of these developments are
reflected in the following passage by the French commentator,
Hippolyte Taine, written in 1862 after a visit to Manchester:

> At about six o'clock the factories discharge an excited,
> noisy crowd into the streets, men, women and children
> swarming in the turgid air. Their clothes are soiled;
> many of the children are bare-footed; the faces are
> drawn and dismal; a number of them stop at the gin-
> shops; the rest scatter to their lairs. We follow them:
> what dreary streets! Through half-open windows we
> could see wretched rooms at ground level, or often
> below the damp earth's surface . . . We pushed on
> towards the suburbs, coming to a more open space
> where rows of small cheap houses have been built
> by speculators. The black streets were paved with
> ironstone slag. Lines of red roofs were ruled against
> the universal grey of the sky. But at least each family
> has its own home, and the fog they breathe there is
> not so contaminated. These are the privileged, the
> fortunate ones. And it is now summer time, the finest
> days of the year! And we wondered what their lives
> must be like in winter, when the fog descends to
> drown, choke, engulf the whole of the visible, natural
> world. And we felt for a moment all the fearful weight
> with which this climate and this industrial system press
> down upon men.
> Walks and visits in the rich quarter of the town.
> Here, and in Liverpool, as in London, the English
> character can be seen in their way of building. The
> townsman does everything in his power to cease being
> a townsman, and tries to fit a country-house and a bit
> of country into a corner of the town. He feels the need
> to be in his own home, to be alone, king of his family
> and servants, and to have about him a bit of park or
> garden in which he can relax after his artificial business

life. From this derives the plan of immense streets, silent and devoid of shops in which each house, surrounded by a plot of green, is isolated and contains only a single family. Furthermore, beyond Manchester lies Bowden, a sort of public villa with a superb park belonging to Lord Stamford who has given the use of it to the public: magnificent trees, rich lawns, herds of half-tame deer lying among the bracken. How men emerging from factory and office must feel all the sweetness and calm of these natural beauties! For in this city . . . even to walk in the rich quarter of the town is depressing. Ten, fifteen, twenty houses in a row built to the same design, one after another like drafts on a drafts-board with mechanical regularity. The well-mowed lawns, the little iron gates and painted façades and symmetrical plots are reminiscent of nice, clean toys. The ornamentation of the houses is in bad taste, capitals, Greek columns, balusters, Gothic roofs and other forms all borrowed from times and places equally remote, all of it fresh and neat and incongruous, an equivocal and trumpery luxury like that of a newly rich self-made man who, trying to look smart, looks bedizened. It is a fine thing to work and an excellent thing to be rich: but to work and be rich are not enough.

Hippolyte Taine, *Notes on England*, trans. Edward Hyams (1957), pp.219–20.

Here the concentric circles of Engels's description have spread beyond the city itself into the surrounding countryside: the workers remain in the shadow of the work-place while, in increasing degrees of affluence, those who order their lives remove themselves from it.

Hearth and Home

Taine's description of the domestic arrangements of the wealthy businessman with its emphasis on family and the comforts of home is anticipated by Mrs Gaskell in her account of the home circumstances of the mill-owner, Carson, in *Mary Barton*. Mrs Gaskell's concern in her first novel was to emphasise the the disparity between the conditions of masters and men: of the 'care-worn men', she says, 'I saw that they were sore and irritable against the rich, the even tenor of whose seemingly happy lives appeared to increase the anguish caused by the lottery-like nature of their own.' (Preface). When she describes the Carson houshold, she draws attention not only to the wealth of which it is a manifestation, but to the culture which wealth makes possible. Like Taine, she points to the position of the father at the head of his household, ministered to by family and servants, and to the civilised leisure of this way of life. The scene is presented in terms of its impact on a working man, who is seeing these things for the first time:

> Mr Carson's was a good house, and furnished with disregard to expense. But in addition to lavish expenditure, there was much taste shown, and many articles chosen for their beauty and elegance adorned his rooms. As Wilson passed a window which a housemaid had thrown open, he saw pictures and gilding, at which he was tempted to stop and look; but then he thought it would not be respectful. So he hastened on to the kitchen door. The servants seemed very busy with preparations for breakfast; but good-naturedly, though hastily, told him to step in, and they could soon let Mr Carson know he was there . . .
>   In the luxurious library, at the well-spread breakfast table, sat the two Mr Carsons, father and son. Both were reading; the father a newspaper, the son a review, while they lazily enjoyed the nicely prepared food. The father was a prepossessing-looking old man; perhaps self-indulgent you might guess. The son was strikingly handsome, and knew it.
>
> *Mary Barton*, Ch. 6.

The rise of a newly affluent industrial and commercial

middle class, living mainly in the cities and with domestic and leisure needs of its own, was a powerful factor in the creation of the Victorian ethic of the family. 'We aspire to live in the Household affections, and to be numbered amongst the Household thoughts, of our readers', Dickens wrote in 1850 in the introductory number of his new periodical, *Household Words*; the title itself, chosen after careful consideration, expresses the intention. Earlier, in *Martin Chuzzlewit* (1843–4), he had satirised the ethic of hearth and home by embodying it in the figure of the fraudulent architect, Seth Pecksniff, whose career is based upon exploitation of the new enthusiasm for domestic architecture. Here he visits the abode of 'perhaps the wealthiest brass and copper founders' family known to mankind',

> . . . a house so big and fierce that its mere outside, like the outside of a giant's castle, struck terror into vulgar minds and made bold persons quail. There was a great front gate; with a great bell, whose handle was in itself a note of admiration; and a great lodge; which being close to the house, rather spoilt the look-out certainly, but made the look-in tremendous.
>
> *Martin Chuzzlewit*, Ch. 9.

Pecksniff is inspired by what he sees to insult the house's owner by offering his professional appraisal of it. This is a London example – the house in question is in Camberwell – but that Pecksniff was a generally topical creation is shown by the founding at this time of journals like *The Architectural Magazine* (1834), and *The Builder* (1844), devoted to the needs created by the rapid expansion of both wealth and population. *The Architectural Magazine* was founded by J. C. Loudon, announced on its title-page as 'Author of *The Encyclopaedia of Cottage, Farm, and Villa Architecture and Furniture*', a work first published in 1833; in the Introduction to the first number it sets out the premises on which it is based:

The study of the science of Architecture recommends

itself to the general reader by the utility of its productions as an art . . . to every individual who either
occupies a house, or intends to occupy one, it will
afford the means of ascertaining what is good or bad
in construction and in appearance, and of choosing,
repairing, altering, fitting up, and furnishing his habitation. Though all men do not build houses, yet all
men in a state of civilisation live in them; and it must,
therefore, be of some importance to every individual,
to have his judgment in the choice of a house heightened
by a knowledge of what points in its construction and
arrangement will contribute most to his security,
convenience and comfort.

The Architectural Magazine and Journal, Vol. I
(1834), pp.1–3.

Loudon follows this up with a broad historical survey and
then directs his attention to those to whom his remarks are
primarily aimed:

To those whose prosperity or fortune enables them to
occupy what are considered good houses, either in
town or country, some knowledge of the science and
practice of Architecture would be not only a source
of perpetual enjoyment, but of real use; because every
accession to our knowledge gives power as well as
pleasure . . . It may be said, indeed, that individuals
so circumstanced as to be able to have handsome
dwellings, can always command the services of professional men to give them advice in the choice or
furnishing of a house.

Ibid.

Loudon's wish to be comprehensive allows him to include
both town and country dwellers in his appeal, just as, like
other architects of his day, he was to concern himself with
problems of working-class accommodation as well as the
needs of the wealthy. But in real terms it was the spending
power of the new middle class which created a new housing

market, and it was in the towns and the cities that this wealth was concentrated. Furthermore, what is implied by Loudon's comment is that this new market was by no means restricted to a small number of the extremely wealthy; it has expanded to a point where it has become a significant influence upon urban development. This is made clear in an account by the American novelist, Nathaniel Hawthorne, of the house he lived in when he was appointed American Consul in Liverpool in 1843. Hawthorne draws attention to the fact that his house is one of many, built on speculation, whereas at home in America such comforts would be available only to 'the very rich'. Most telling of all is his indication of the precautions taken to ensure the privacy of the occupants who are protected not only by a toll charged to pass through the street but by the employment of a policeman to enforce it:

> We got into our new house in Rock Park, yesterday. It is quite a good house, with three apartments, besides kitchen and pantry, on the lower; and three stories high, with four good chambers in each story. It is a stone edifice, like almost all the modern English houses, and handsome in its design – much more so than most of the American houses. The rent, without furniture, would probably have been £100; – furnished, it is £160. Rock Park, as the locality is called, is private property, and is now nearly covered with residences for professional people, merchants, and others of the upper middling class; the houses being mostly built, I suppose, on speculation, and let to those who occupy them. It is the quietest place imaginable; there being a police station at the entrance; and the officer on duty admits no ragged or ill looking person to pass. There being a toll, it precludes all unnecessary passage of carriages; and never were there more noiseless streets than those which give access to these pretty residences. On either side, there is thick shrubbery, with glimpses through it at the ornamented portals, or into the trim gardens, with smooth shaven lawns, of no large extent, but still affording reasonable breathing space. They really are an improvement on anything save what the

very rich can enjoy, in America. The former occupants
. . . of our house having been fond of flowers, there
are many rare varieties in the garden; and we are told
that there is scarcely a month of the year in which a
flower will not be found there.

> Nathaniel Hawthorne, *English Notebooks*, ed.
> Randall Stewart (1962), p.22.

Where the lower classes were concerned, housing conditions were seen as a major problem of urbanisation. Articles
on the problem of working-class housing in the cities figured
frequently in the architectural journals and also in works like
H. Roberts's *The Dwellings of the Labouring Poor* (1850)
and Cheyne Brady's *The Practicability of Improving the
Dwellings of the Labouring Poor* (1859). In 1844 the Society
for Improving the Condition of the Labouring Classes was
founded, to be followed by the Metropolitan Society for
Improving the Dwellings of the Industrial Classes in the
following year. But, as their dates might suggest, these were
responses to an already overwhelming need: admirable as
their motivation may have been, the sheer size of the problem
meant that there was little in practical terms that such
initiatives could achieve. Lacking the economic power to
provide for more than basic necessities, the lower classes were
inevitably forced into over-crowded, unhealthy and generally
inadequate accommodation. Furthermore, if middle-class concern was widespread, it often expressed itself in terms of
a moral self-righteousness which suggested only limited
understanding of the realities. In the following example, a
contemporary commentator, G. R. Porter, after noting the
'improvement [in] the condition of the dwellings of the middle
classes', goes on to consider the less fortunate members of
society:

> The improvement here noticed has not hitherto been
> extended in an equal degree to the dwellings of the
> working classes. These, especially in large towns,
> are still for the most part comfortless, and even
> unwholesome, ill furnished and ill kept, betraying a

lamentable want of self-respect in their inmates, with a degree of recklessness that speaks unfavourably for their moral progress.

> G. R. Porter, *The Progress of the Nation* (1847, new edn 1851), pp.522–3.

The situation, he notices, is not uniform, and he identifies Sheffield as a town which exemplifies what can be achieved by a self-respecting working-class. Sheffield, he notes, 'contains a large manufacturing population, by no means remarkable for orderly conduct.' Nevertheless its working population seem to provide themselves with the basic decencies of family life:

> . . . it is the custom for each family among the labouring population to occupy a separate dwelling, the rooms in which are furnished in a very comfortable manner, the floors are carpeted, and the tables are usually of mahogany; chests of drawers of the same material are commonly seen, and so in most cases is a clock also, the possession of which article of furniture has often been pointed out as the certain indication of prosperity and of personal respectability on the part of the working man.

> Ibid.

Porter confesses himself unable to account for 'this favourable pecularity' which he has observed in Sheffield, but the instance is not as isolated as his attitude would seem to suggest. In *Mary Barton* Mrs Gaskell observes that working-class life-styles reflect the cycle of trade; in good times the good workman lives well but when times are bad he is vulnerable. At the opening of the novel she describes the home of John Barton, her working-class hero:

> The place seemed almost crammed with furniture (sure sign of good times among the mills). Beneath the window was a dresser with three deep drawers. Opposite the fire-place was a table, which I should call a Pembroke, only that it was made of deal, and I

cannot tell how such a name may be applied to such
humble material. On it, resting against the wall, was
a bright green japanned tea-tray, having a couple of
scarlet lovers embracing in the middle. The fire-light
danced merrily on this, and really (setting all taste but
that of a child's aside) it gave a richness of colouring
to that side of the room.

Mary Barton, Ch. 2.

These details are confirmed in a description of working-class
housing in Manchester by the journalist, Angus Bethune
Reach, in one of the articles he contributed to the *Morning
Chronicle* in 1849. Reach, like Porter, instances the clock as
a particularly significant item:

In most cases the doors of the houses stand hospitably
open, and young children cluster over the thresholds
and swarm out upon the pavement: you thus have an
easy opportunity of noting the interiors as you pass
along. They are, as you will perceive, a series of little
rooms, about ten feet by eight, more or less, generally
floored with brick or flagstones – materials which are,
however, occasionally half concealed by strips of mats
or faded carpeting. A substantial deal table stands in
the centre of each apartment, and a few chairs, stools,
and settles to match, are ranged around. Occasionally
a little table of mahogany is not wanting. Now
and then you observe a curiously small sofa, hardly
intended for a full grown man or woman to stretch
their limbs upon; and about as often one side of the
fireplace is taken up with a cradle. Sometimes there is
a large cupboard, the open door of which reveals a
shining assortment of plates and dishes; sometimes the
humble dinner service is ranged on shelves which
stretch along the walls; while beneath them is suspended upon hooks a more or less elaborate series of
skillets, stewpans, and miscellaneous cooking and
household matters. A conspicuous object is very frequently a painted and highly-glazed tea tray, upon

which the firelight glints cheerily, and which, by
its superior lustre and artistic boldness of design,
commonly throws into the shade the couple or so
of tiny prints, in narrow black frames, which are
suspended above it. A favourite, and no doubt useful
article of furniture is a clock. No Manchester operative
will be without one a moment longer than he can help.

> Angus Bethune Reach, *Manchester and the
> Textile Districts in 1849*, ed. C. Aspin (1972), pp.6–7.

While commentators like Porter had obvious reasons for
enjoining the working classes to self-help and respectability,
both Gaskell's novel and Reach's journalism serve to show
that the idea of working-class respectability was not in itself
a bourgeois myth. The homes they describe though are those
of the more affluent and established workers: for the less
fortunate, and in particular for the itinerant or vagrant city-
dwellers, conditions were altogether less favourable. Amongst
the worst living conditions were those to be found in the
lodging houses, often situated in the most impoverished areas
in the cities. Reach describes some lodging-houses he visited
in 'the lowest, most filthy, most unhealthy, and most wicked
locality in Manchester':

We first went into an ordinary 'low lodging house'.
The hour, I should state, was about nine o'clock at
night. A stout man, partially undressed, was sitting,
nursing a child, upon the bed of the outer room,
and the landlady emerged from the inner apartment,
whence followed her a great clack of male and female
tongues. The woman spoke with profound deference
to my companion, and began to assure him that the
house was the best conducted in all Manchester.
Meanwhile we had entered the inner room. It was a
stiflingly hot place, with a large fire, over which
flickered a rush-light, or very small candle, stuck in a
greased tin sconce. There were eight or ten men and
women seated on stools and low chairs round the fire
. . . The beds upstairs were broken and rickety, and

[sic] clothes which were bundles of brown rags. These couches were placed so close that you could only just make your way between them . . .

The nominal price of fourpence for a bed I found to be everywhere the same, and the general disposition of the bedrooms was equally identical. They consist simply of filthy unscoured chambers, with stained and discoloured walls, scribbled over with names and foul expressions. There was no article of furniture other than the beds – not even, so far as I saw, a chest. Still the worst of the places was quite water-tight.

Reach, op. cit., pp.54–5.

There were those yet more disadvantaged than the lodging-house residents. As Reach goes on to say, 'There were few or no Irish in the houses we had just visited. They live in more wretched places still – the cellars.' The cellar-dwellers, of which to a varying degree each of the industrial cities had its share, were literally and metaphorically at the bottom of the pile. Again, *Mary Barton* provides us with a fictional example: in Chapter 6 of her novel Mrs Gaskell takes us to the home of a sick worker, no longer able to work, and living with his family in a room mainly below ground. He is visited by two of his work-mates:

You went down one step even from the foul area into the cellar in which a family of human beings lived. It was very dark inside. The window-panes were many of them broken and stuffed with rags, which was reason enough for the dusky light that pervaded the place even at mid-day. After the account I have given of the state of the street, no one can be surprised that on going into the cellar inhabited by Davenport, the smell was so foetid as almost to knock the two men down. Quickly recovering themselves, as those inured to such things do, they began to penetrate the thick darkness of the place, and to see three or four little children rolling on the damp, nay wet, brick floor, through which the stagnant, filthy moisture of the street oozed up; the fire-place was empty and blank; the wife sat on her husband's chair, and cried in the dank loneliness.

Mary Barton, Ch. 6.

This fictional account can be authenticated by reference to the evidence submitted to the various parliamentary committees charged with investigating conditions in the towns and cities in the 1840s. Amongst the most distressing of this evidence was that relating to Liverpool. We have earlier cited the account of middle-class housing in Liverpool by Nathaniel Hawthorne. By an interesting coincidence Hawthorne had been preceded in Liverpool by his great compatriot, Herman Melville, who in his autobiographical novel *Redburn*, recorded the impact made upon him by seeing the most extreme conditions of poverty in the same city:

Once, passing through this place, I heard a feeble wail, which seemed to me to come out of the earth. It was but a strip of crooked sidewalk where I stood; the dingy wall was on every side, converting the mid-day into twilight; and not a soul was in sight. I started, and could almost have run, when I heard that dismal sound. It seemed the low, endless wail of someone forever lost. At last I advanced to an opening which communicated downward with deep tiers of cellars beneath a crumbling old warehouse; and there, some fifteen feet below the walk, crouching in nameless squalor, with her head bowed over, was the figure of what had been a woman. Her blue arms folded to her livid bosom two shrunken things like children, that leaned toward her, one on each side. At first I knew not whether they were alive or dead. They made no sign; they did not move or stir; but from the vault came that soul-sickening wail . . .

They were dumb and next to dead with want. How they had crawled into that den I could not tell; but there they had crawled to die. At that moment I never thought of relieving them; for death was so stamped

in their glazed and unimploring eyes that I already
regarded them as already no more. I stood looking
down on them, while my whole soul swelled within
me; and I asked myself, What right had anybody in
the wide world to smile and be glad, when sights like
this were to be seen? . . .

At last, I walked on towards an open lot in the alley,
hoping to meet there some ragged old women, whom
I had daily noticed groping amid foul rubbish for little
particles of dirty cotton, which they washed out and
sold for a trifle . . .

I found them; and accosting one, I asked if she knew
of the persons I had just left. She replied, that she did
not, nor did she want to. I then asked another, a
miserable, toothless old woman, with a tattered strip
of coarse baling stuff round her body. Looking at me
for an instant, she resumed her raking in the rubbish,
and said that she knew who it was that I spoke of; but
that she had not time to attend to beggars and their
brats. Accosting still another, who seemed to know
my errand, I asked if there was no place to which the
woman could be taken. 'Yes,' she replied, 'to the
churchyard.' I said she was alive and not dead.

Herman Melville, *Redburn* (1839), Ch. 37.

What is surely most chilling in this account is the rejection
of the destitute family by their own kind. When Redburn
tries to involve a policeman in the situation, he is curtly told
that it is none of his business. To Melville, as to Hawthorne,
the policeman is significant: he is there to ensure that divisions
in this urban society shall not disturb its peace.

Public Health

The most drastic consequences of the expansion of the urban
population in the first half of the nineteenth century were its
effects upon public health. While the middle and upper classes
were able to ensure for themselves a reasonable degree of

living space, for the lower classes intense over-crowding in accommodation often unfit for habitation, largely non-existent sanitary arrangements and the concomitant environmental hazards of the new industrialism ensured that they were never free from the threat of endemic disease.

In 1848 the journalist and popular poet Charles Mackay published a poem, 'The Mowers', to which he gave the sub-title 'An Anticipation of the Cholera'. From 1835 to 1844 Mackay had been assistant sub-editor of *The Morning Chronicle*, and in 1849 he was to contribute reports on Liverpool and Birmingham to its series of articles on the condition of the industrial poor throughout Britain. His poem is a strange production. With a menacing but unspecified city setting – 'Dense on the stream the vapours lay,/Thick as wool on the cold highway;/Spongy and dim each lonely lamp/Shone o'er the streets so dull and damp' – it reports in direct speech the prophecies of three 'Spectres', each of which boasts of its destructive powers. The last and most terrifying of these apparitions is the spectre of disease:

'I brew disease in stagnant pools,
    And wandering here, disporting there,
Favoured much by knaves and fools,
    I poison streams, I taint the air;
I shake from my locks the spreading pest,
I keep the typhus at my behest;
In filth and slime
I crawl, I climb,
I find the workman at his trade,
    I blow on his lips and down he lies;
I look in the face of the ruddiest maid,
    And straight the fire forsakes her eyes –
    She droops, she sickens, and she dies;
I stint the growth of babes new born
Or shear them off like standing corn;
I rob the sunshine of its glow,
I poison all the winds that blow;
Whenever they pass they suck my breath
And freight their wings with certain death.

'Tis *I* am the lord of the crowded town –
I mow them down, I mow them down!'

Even this most terrible force, though, must yield pride of
place to the greatest threat of all:

'But great as we are, there cometh one
    Greater than you – greater than I,
To aid the deeds that shall be done,
To end the work that we've begun,
    And thin this thick humanity.
I see his footmarks east and west,
    I hear his tread in the silence fall,

'He shall not sleep, he shall not rest –
    He comes to aid us one and all.
Were men as wise as men might be,
They would not work for you, for me,
For him that cometh over the sea;
But they will not heed the warning voice.
The Cholera comes, rejoice! rejoice!
He shall be lord of the swarming town,
And mow them down, and mow them down!'

Charles Mackay, 'The Mowers', Town Lyrics and
Other Poems (1848), pp.37–41.

Mackay's poem is an indictment of those who resisted
legislation designed to alleviate the public health problems of
the cities. In distinguishing cholera from disease in general it
recognises its symbolic as well as its factual significance.
Cholera was, of course, a virulent epidemic disease which
struck twice – the first time in 1831 and the second in 1848 –
in the first half of the nineteenth century. Far more persistent,
and in terms of the mortality they caused statistically more
significant, were the respiratory diseases, most notably tuber-
culosis. But cholera, coming as it was known to have done
from abroad, was seen as an avenging destroyer. The epidemic
of 1831 was first detected in Sunderland, at that time the
fourth biggest port in Britain: the anxiety about its potential

led to the setting up, albeit temporarily, of a central Board of Health for the first time, and the decades of the thirties and forties were thereafter to be distinguished by a series of official enquiries and reports directed towards public health legislation. Anticipating these was James Kay's *The Moral and Physical Condition of the Working Classes Employed in the Cotton Manufacture in Manchester* in which he wrote,

> Notwithstanding the general knowledge which the manufacturers must have of the condition of the working classes, yet, before the appearance of the Cholera, they were not so well convinced as they now are, that the minute interference of the higher ranks is necessary to the physical and moral elevation of the poor.
>
> James Kay, *The Moral and Physical Condition of the Working Classes* (1832, reprinted 1969), p.11.

Kay's study was followed by other similar enterprises, and above all by the famous 'Blue Books' – the reports of the parliamentary select committees and the royal commissions – amongst the most notable of which were the *Report of the Select Committee on the Health of Towns* (1840), the *Report on the Sanitary Condition of the Labouring Population* by Edwin Chadwick (1842) and the two *Report(s) of the Royal Commission for Inquiring into the State of Large Towns and Populous Districts* (1844 and 1845).

These reports give us a unique insight into the prevailing conditions in the towns and cities at this period. Scrupulously precise in their documentation, and explicit in their detail, they shock by the very clinical detachment of their analysis. Here, for example, is an extended account of housing conditions in Birmingham – a city with apparent advantages – in 1845:

> Birmingham, containing 189,000 inhabitants, is perhaps one of the most healthy of our large towns. It possesses many natural advantages – as a good site,

with adequate fall for drainage, a dry and porous sub-soil, and water generally of good quality. A good and cheap supply of coal is found in the vicinity . . .

The principal streets of Birmingham are generally wide, well made and with sufficient fall; in the parish of Birmingham the drains in the main streets are well laid and tolerably attended to. The houses of the richer and middle classes are generally dry and airy, and with convenient buildings appendant to them. The supply of water for these classes is good, and the drainage and cleansing is little complained of, though susceptible of considerable improvement.

The state of habitations of the working and poorer classes is often widely different. Their houses vary indeed greatly in comfort and convenience, as in size and situation, and the excellent custom of each family having a house to themselves appears generally to prevail. I am obliged however reluctantly to say, that many, if not most of the narrow streets, alleys and courts in which their habitations are situated, are much neglected as regards drainage, paving and cleansing, and though wells are found in most of them, they are frequently out of order, or the water indifferent.

The courts in the parish of Birmingham alone are above 2,000 in number, and their inhabitants exceed 50,000; besides many in the adjacent parish of Aston. "The ingress to most of the courts is by a narrow entry, from three to four feet in width. This is generally arched and built over, so as to form part of the houses fronting the street. The ventilation of the court is by this narrow and covered state of the entry very much impeded." The number of houses in each court varies from four or five to 20 or 30. At the end, or on one side, there is often a washhouse, sometimes an ash-pit, and always one or two privies, or sets of privies, close to which there is often one or more pig-sties, tubs full of hog-wash, and heaps of offensive manure. In the midst of the court stands the pump of supply for the inhabitants. These courts are frequently unpa-ved, and the open channel ill-defined, so that stagnant puddles in wet weather are the consequence.

In many, the overflowings from the privy vaults, pigsties and dirt heaps, trickling down the court, pass close to the well, and no doubt often enter it. Many of these courts are unpaved. There appears to be no system of sweeping or cleansing of any kind, except what is from time to time done by the inhabitants themselves. The smaller streets are also much neglected in this respect; and this remark applies to every town visited.

In Birmingham, and in many of the towns around it, the privies belonging to the houses of the working classes, and many others, are constructed in almost all cases with open vaults for the night-soil at the back or side of the building. These are not covered over with either stone, wood, or earth, but exhale continually a most offensive stench. They are sometimes fenced round with a low wall, but often left quite open. In either case, ashes, stalks of vegetables, and other refuse, are thrown in, and the mass is left to taint the air from month to month. In rainy weather this receptacle of filth often overflows, and traces its fetid course through the open channel of the court or alley, and along the pathway entrance, till it reaches the street.

The Report of the former Committee on the State of Birmingham said with great truth, 'There appears in general to be no drainage for the privies by which their more fluid contents might pass away'; and adds 'the privies and ash-pits in the courts in our opinion require regular inspection and cleansing.'

The neglect of all public regulations for draining, cleansing, or paving the courts and alleys in which the poorer classes reside, prevails in all the towns and districts visited . . .

I believe the consequences of this neglect . . . to be most injurious to the health of the people – to be inimical to cleanliness, decency, and habits of self-respect, so beneficial to all classes.

Second Report of the Commission for Inquiring

into Large Towns and Populous Districts (1845);
Parliamentary Papers, Vol. XVIII, pp.133–5.

This report makes the point that we find emphasised by the
novelists: there is an enormous gulf between the classes
reflected by their living conditions. Furthermore the commissioner is not inhibited by the kind of constraints imposed
upon the imaginative writers. In his emphasis on the problems
arising from inadequate arrangements for water supply, and
for drainage and sewage disposal, he indicates in very clear
detail the realities that lie behind their allusions. When Mrs
Gaskell, for example, refers to 'household slops of *every*
description' being tossed into the gutter (*Mary Barton*, Ch.
6), her readers would have taken the point of her emphasis: in
Bleak House (1852–3) Dickens was to represent the condition
of England by the symbolism of disease.

Bleak House has as one of its focal symbolic locations the
burial-ground to which Jo the crossing-sweeper brings the
aristocratic Lady Dedlock in search of her long-dead lover.
The problem of the disposal of the dead was the most macabre
expression of the consequences of over-crowding in the cities,
and in 1843 it occasioned a government report of its own.
The city burial-grounds and churchyards, already filled with
the dead of centuries, could scarcely be expected to accommodate a further influx. Attempts to fill them to the point of
overflowing not only offended religious sensibilities, they
were in themselves a further threat to public health. At the
same time, the increasing popularity amongst the wealthier
classes of elaborate funeral rituals – in itself an expression of
the developing cult of the family – facilitated the development
of prestigious private cemeteries. In death, as in life, the
Victorian city-dwellers were very definitely divided. All of
these developments are reflected in the following passage:

> The information obtained by correspondence from
> Edinburgh, Glasgow, Bristol, Birmingham, Coventry,
> and several towns in Ireland, tends to the conclusion
> that the leading principles set forth in this report are
> applicable to all crowded town districts, with but few
> modifications. In all the practice of interment in towns,

the crowded state of the place of burial, the apparent
want of seclusion and sanctity pollute the mental
associations, and offend the sentiments of the population, irrespective of any considerations of public
health; in almost all, this state of feeling is manifested
by the increasing resort of persons of the higher and
middle classes to such cemeteries as have been formed
out of the towns by private individuals who have
associated, and taken advantage of the feelings to
procure subscriptions for the formation of more accept-
able places of sepulture . . . In nearly all the towns
where the graveyards are crowded by the burials of an
increasing population, evidence was tendered of the
outrages perpetrated upon the feelings of the population by the gravediggers in the disposal of undecompo-
sed remains to make space for new interments . . . In
all the populous provincial towns the need of the
superior superintendence of the material arrangements
for interment, and the exercise of such functions as
those described as falling to a superior officer of public
health, appear to be even more urgent than in the
metropolis.

Supplementary Report on the Results of a Special
Inquiry into the Practice of Interment in Towns
(1843), *Parliamentary Papers*, Vol. XII, pp.573–4.

'Regulation', 'superior superintendence': the accounts of
the official investigators, together with those of the crusading
journalists and the social-problem novelists all pointed
towards some form of central organisation for the alleviation
of the conditions they exposed. Diagnosis, however, was to
prove easier than legislative cure, for attempts to legislate
for improvements invariably came up against entrenched
opposition. In that any solution inevitably involved interference with private property, landowners were likely to feel an
imposition on their rights. Furthermore there was as yet no
consistent system of local government, answerable to central
authority; such improvements as could be set in motion could
operate only at a local level, and as a result of individual

initiative. In Liverpool, for example, the local Corporation opened baths and wash-houses in 1842; elsewhere private schemes for improved housing set an example that others might follow. But reform at the behest of government conflicted with what Nassau Senior called 'the principle of non-interference': this finds expression in an article in *The Economist*, published in the aftermath of an influenza epidemic and in anticipation of the cholera outbreak of 1848. Dickens, in a famous passage in *Bleak House*, was to ask, 'What connexion can there have been between many people in the innumerable histories of this world, who, from opposite sides of great gulfs, have, nevertheless, been very curiously brought together!' (*Bleak House*, Ch. 16). The writer in *The Economist* begins by proposing an answer to this question of 'connexion':

> It is a remarkable sign of the changes which have taken place in society that some of the upper classes now occupy themselves with sewers and cesspools . . . The mode in which this is brought about establishes a close connexion between the extreme classes of society. The very poorest become, from foul drains, the prey of fever; from them fever, with its ghastly aspect, threatens the very opulent. They cannot hope to escape a general epidemic; at any rate they are called on to support the sick poor, and they thus become personally interested in the preservation of their health.

> *The Economist*, Vol. V, No. 224, 11 December 1847.

This is an exact prediction of what happens in *Bleak House*, where the heroine, Esther Summerson, is contaminated by smallpox, contracted as a direct result of her care for the social outcast, Jo. Nevertheless, *The Economist* concludes its article with an explicit rejection of government intervention:

> It is especially necessary, we think, to be cautious when the community is afflicted by one disease, and is apprehensive of another, not to allow alarm to banish reason, and promote to a vast extent that

interference of Government which is obviously burden-
ing it day after day with a responsibility too great for
human beings.

Ibid.

It was because of attitudes such as this that when the first
Public Health Act was passed in 1848 it proved to be only a
temporary measure. It created a central Board of Health, in
the first instance for five years, but with limited and mainly
permissive powers. Although these powers were renewed for
a further year, the Board ceased to function in 1854, and *The
Times* responded as if a victory had been won:

> The Board of Health has fallen . . . we prefer to take
> our chance of cholera and the rest than be bullied into
> health . . .
> There is nothing so much a man hates as being cleansed
> against his will, or having his floors swept, his walls
> whitewashed, his pet dunghills cleared away, or his
> thatch forced to give way for slate, all at the command
> of a sort of sanitary bumbailiff.

The Times, 1 August 1854.

Attempts to deal with public health problems then reverted
to piecemeal legislation to tackle individual problems or to
local initiatives with few guiding principles and no central
control. Thus an account of Birmingham in 1857 suggest that
little had changed since 1845 (see pp.56–8). If anything,
indeed, matters had become worse, given a greater degree of
industrial pollution and the proliferation of outlets for the
sale of alcohol in the intervening decade:

> The causes – the removable causes – which appear
> to be most active in Birmingham in increasing the rate
> of mortality, are the following:
> The evolution of various gases which are disengaged
> in such processes as bone-boiling, the preparation of
> artificial manures, from knackers'-yards, slaughter-
> houses, pig-styes, &c.

The present method of removing night-soil and other impurities by means of carts and wagons, a plan rendered necessary by the absence of house drainage; and by which deleterious gases are nightly very extensively diffused through the atmosphere.

The smoke emitted in such immense volumes from the numberless manufactures with which the town abounds, constantly clouding the atmosphere, and interfering, as every inhabitant can testify, with the healthy functions of the animal economy.

Lastly, a prolific source of disease will be found in the extreme facility afforded to the poor and labouring classes for obtaining unwholesome compounds, in the shape of beer and spirits, in which so large a portion of their hard-earned gains is expended, to the exclusion of the proper necessaries of life for themselves and families. The vast increase in the number of beer-houses and spirit-vaults has had a most pernicious influence both in swelling our tables of mortality, and in facilitating the first steps to crime.

> Thomas Green, 'The Mortality of Birmingham
> Compared with that of Seven Other Towns',
> *Transactions of the National Association for the
> Promotion of Social Science* (1857) pp.362–3.

It was not until the publication of the reports of the Royal Sanitary Commission in 1871 that it was finally established that the creation of healthy living conditions was the responsibility of central government, and that, in the words of the commissioners, 'the present fragmentary and confused Sanitary legislation should be consolidated, and . . . the administration of Sanitary Law should be made uniform, universal, and imperative throughout the kingdom'. (*Second Report of the Royal Sanitary Commission*, 1871, *Parliamentary Papers*, Vol. XXXV, p.3.) Since we have drawn much of our evidence from the city of Birmingham in this section it is right to record that it was Birmingham, under the leadership of Joseph Chamberlain in the decade that was to follow, which set an example to the cities in matters of public government and planning. (See Asa Briggs, *Victorian Cities*, Ch. 5). It was only once the principle of corporate responsibility had been established at government level that the cities could initiate the large-scale measures necessary for comprehensive reform.

3 Social Control

Municipal Government

The expansion of the urban communities, both physically and in terms of their density of population, raised the central issue of how they were to be governed. From the early nineteenth century it became clear that a system of local government which had evolved to serve the needs of a predominantly rural society would not be adequate to cope with the conditions created by the new industrialism. The ethos of the new communities was essentially individualistic, but whatever reservations there might be about the threat to individual freedoms of imposed legislation, the fact that *laissez-faire* would not on its own solve the problems created by urban expansion was inescapable. *Laissez-faire* itself was in fact only one half of a paradoxical equation: Benthamite utilitarianism was the predominant philosophy of Victorian commercial achievement and by its token administrative reform was a necessary requirement to ensure the efficient workings of the new social machine. Even a Romantic anti-Benthamite like Carlyle called unequivocally for legislation to solve society's problems:

> Again, are not Sanitary Regulations possible for a Legislature? The old Romans had their Aediles; who would, I think, in direct contravention to supply-and-demand, have rigorously seen rammed into total abolition many a foul cellar in our Southwarks, Saint-Gileses, and dark poison-lanes; saying sternly, 'Shall a Roman man dwell there?' The Legislature, at whatever cost of consequences, would have had to answer, 'God forbid!' – The Legislature, even as it now is, could order all dingy Manufacturing Towns to cease from their soot and darkness; to let-in the blessed sunlight, the blue of Heaven, and become clear and clean; to

burn their coal-smoke, namely, and make flame of it. Baths, free air, a wholesome temperature, ceilings twenty feet high, might be ordained, by Act of Parliament, in all establishments licensed as Mills. There are such Mills already extant; – honour to the builders of them! The Legislators can say to others: Go ye and do likewise; better, if you can.

Every toiling Manchester, its smoke and soot all burnt, ought it not, among so many world-wide conquests, to have a hundred acres or so of free greenfield, with trees on it, conquered, for its little children to disport in; for its all-conquering workers to take a breath of twilight air in? You would say so! A willing Legislature could say so with effect. A willing Legislature could say very many things! And to whatsoever 'vested interests', or suchlike, stood up, gainsaying merely, 'I shall lose profits,' – the willing Legislature would answer, 'Yes, but my sons and daughters will gain health, and life, and a soul.' – 'What is to become of our invaluable Cotton-trade?' cried certain Spinners, when the Factory Bill was proposed; The Humanity of England answered steadfastly: 'Deliver me these rickety perishing souls of infants, and let your Cotton-trade take its chance. God Himself commands the one thing; not God especially the other thing. We cannot have prosperous Cotton-trades at the expense of keeping the Devil a partner in them!'

> Thomas Carlyle, *Past and Present* (1843), Bk IV, Ch. 3.

Carlyle was never less than sceptical of schemes of democratic reform: his 'Legislature' is conceived as an entirely autocratic body. But his rhetoric here identifies the conflict between the powers of government and the claims of private interests, and comes out without qualification on the side of intervention. Carlyle would have objected to the agency by which they were achieved, but the specific benefits he calls for – pollution control, improved factory conditions, and the provision of public parks and open spaces in the hearts of the cities – were to feature prominently amongst the concerns of Victorian government.

The investigations of the various Parliamentary commissions of the early 1840s were to lead to legislation at national level. The growth of the cities though had focussed the already existing problems of local government. Just as the Reform Act of 1832 had provided for the reorganisation of parliamentary government, recognising both shifts in population and the need for an extended suffrage, so it was conceded that at municipal level reform was necessary. Systems of local government which had developed pragmatically over the centuries could no longer be adequate to the needs of the new communities. An indication of the problem as it affected the Manchester area is given in a contemporary history:

> The rapid rise of Manchester and Salford in opulence and population, as well as in political and commercial importance, renders it an interesting enquiry, under what local government and municipal regulations that elevation in the scale of the empire has been attained. The enquiry will show that these towns are governed by the same authority as when the countless streets were subjected to the plough; when their manufactures originated with the distaff, and when their traffic was conveyed on the backs of horses to 'London and Sturbich [Stourbridge] Fayres'. And yet that mass of buildings, which to a stranger appears one town, and is in common parlance so called and considered, and which consists of the several townships of Manchester, Salford, Ardwick, Cheetham, Chorlton Row, Hulme, and Pendleton, comprehending 157,751 inhabitants, has no greater authority within its immense population, than that which preserves the peace of the most insignificant village. By their respective charters Manchester and Salford are ancient boroughs, but they have no corporation, nor do they have any burgesses in Parliament.
>
> Edward Baines, *History of the County Palatine of Lancaster* (1831), Vol. II, pp.151–2.

Baines's reference to the preservation of the peace is an indication of the fact that for many anxieties about social stability were the main motive for reform: to that extent local government and the preservation of law and order are seen to be synonymous. The point was made explicitly by Sir Robert Peel, arguing for corporation reform in the parliamentary debate on the Municipal Corporations Act of 1835:

> Sir, when I look to the state of the population of the larger towns of this kingdom – when I contemplate the rapidity with which places, which at no remote period were inconsiderable villages, have through manufacturing industry, started into life and into great wealth and importance – when I look, too, to the imperfect provision which is now made for the preservation of order and administration of justice in most of those towns – I cannot deny that the time has arrived when it is of the utmost importance to the well-being of society, to establish within societies so circumstanced a good system of Municipal government.
>
> *Hansard*, Vol. XXVIII, (22 May to 26 June 1835), col.559.

Peel goes on to argue that it is only by a reformed system of government that 'the regular and pure administration of justice may be extended and secured, and the maintainence of public order promoted through the means of a well-regulated police.' Once established, a reformed system of local government was to concern itself with far more than policing, and the impulse towards social control was to find expression through various agencies. Peel's comments, however, make it very clear why the need for an efficient system of government in the industrial cities was felt to be so urgent.

As with other nineteenth-century reforms, the symbolic significance of the Municipal Corporations Act should not lead us to exaggerate its practical effect. Prior to 1835 local government had been invested in three major agencies: the Corporations, three-quarters of which were 'closed' – that is, unelected – the Parish Vestries, and the Improvement Commissions. The main effects of the Act were to replace the closed institutions by elective bodies with precisely defined powers, and to introduce a more systematic local electoral system with annual elections and, subject to certain qualifications, equal household franchise. At the same time there was a number of appointed bodies – Boards of Guardians, for example – to deal with specific issues and problems. The 'Board' before whom Oliver Twist appeared, 'very sage, deep, philosophical men' (Dickens, *Oliver Twist*, 1838, Ch. 2), who apply their utilitarian principles so efficiently in the administration of the workhouse was just such a body. It cannot be said that the 1835 Act produced any automatic increase in efficiency. Much of the work of the old-style Improvement Commissions was more effective than that of the elected bodies and can be said to have anticipated later developments. Aspects of the old order would seem in some cases to have survived the new system, while holders of local office, whether elected or not, were often lacking in experience and ability. But, as with parliamentary reform, holders of public office were at least in principle democratically accountable and, by the same token, public office could be seen to bring recognition and distinction. The towns and cities were now in theory at least responsible for their own governance, and civic pride became an increasing factor of public consciousness.

Dickens, as might be expected, was from the first an opponent of the pretensions of holders of public office, although many of his targets are technically speaking figures of the pre-Reform and small-town England in which he himself grew up. The Board of Guardians in *Oliver Twist* is for him an unusually explicit contemporary subject of satire: more typical perhaps is the mayor of Eatanswill in the following scene from *Pickwick Papers*:

'Silence,' roared the mayor's attendants.
'Whiffin, proclaim silence,' said the mayor, with an

air of pomp befitting his lofty station. In obedience to this command the crier performed another concerto on the bell, whereupon a gentleman in the crowd called out 'muffins;' which occasioned another laugh.

'Gentlemen,' said the Mayor, at as loud a pitch as he could possibly force his voice to, 'Gentlemen. Brother electors of the Borough of Eatanswill. We are met here to-day, for the purpose of choosing a representative in the room of our late –'

Here the Mayor was interrupted by a voice from the crowd.

'Suc-cess to the Mayor!' cried the voice, 'and may he never desert the nail and sarspan business, as he got his money by.'

Charles Dickens, *Pickwick Papers* (1836–7), Ch. 13.

The events of *Pickwick Papers* are set in the years immediately preceding the 1832 Reform Act and predominantly in rural England, but it can justifiably be argued that the Eatanswill election reflects the abuses of the post-Reform scene. Certainly Dickens makes much of the iniquities of the polarisation of politics on party lines, a factor which a contemporary commentator, Sir Charles Shaw, at one time Police Commissioner for Manchester, held to be responsible for the poor quality of the elected government of Manchester in the period following the Municipal Corporations Act. 'In October 1839,' Shaw wrote, 'Manchester, as far as its local government was concerned, was in a most disorganised and disunited state, owing to local political animosity.' (*Replies of Sir Charles Shaw to Lord Ashley, M.P. regarding the Education, and Moral and Physical Condition of the Labouring Classes*, 1843, reprinted in *The Factory Education Bill of 1843: Six Pamphlets*, 1972, Part 1, p.5.) Party populism, indeed, threatened to nullify the beneficial effects of reform, leading, for example, to appeals to self-interest and particularly to economy, that undermined the larger and often costly needs of the communities. An interesting indication of what were undoubtedly common attitudes towards civic dignitaries is

offered in a long poem about Birmingham, published by a
local author, Harry H. Horton, in 1851:

> But stop, my muse – of reckless haste beware,
> Have we not got a Council and a Mayor?
> A local parliament, where men are found
> To rise at once like mushrooms from the ground,
> And get to office as the dream of each,
> Weening the chair within his easy reach;
> But even Mayors, strange as it seems, are made
> *To order*, like an article of trade:
> The man who sits unnoticed and alone,
> Unswayed by parties, and to cliques unknown
> Will never rise upon the breath of fame,
> Nor leave in councils a remembered name;
> But he that only talks, no matter what,
> And leads (however small) a factious knot –
> Who substitutes for principle and sense
> Some selfish aim or arrogant pretence,
> Soon, soon attains the long-wished-for renown,
> And lives his day, the hero of the town.
> But now the Council, with new members strong,
> Boasts, too, its earnest enemies of wrong;
> Amongst whose band in justice must be placed
> One who his antecedents has effaced
> By deeds which o'er-taxed poverty must prize
> As rate and levies year by year arise:
> The parish bills and wants he seems to know
> And nought escapes the Argus-eyes of J—:
> But, still untir'd, his daring soul would aim
> To fill each place, and ev'ry honour claim:
> And, like some greedy monster of the deep,
> From whose approach the little fishes, sweep,
> Methinks I see him, unabashed, prepare
> To grace, as ne'er was graced, the civic chair.
> But let us not to merit be unkind,
> Or to the talents of the rich be blind.
> There are amongst those *nobs* of lowly birth –
> Men who have risen by intrinsic worth:
> Men, who from measuring tapes, or selling gin,

Have onward pushed, some added wealth to win:
Who, still aspiring, yet would not disdain
To lend a hand that others too might gain
The height themselves have reached – and who would
spare
Time, labour, love, on aught that promised fair.

Harry H. Horton, *Birmingham: a Poem* (1851).

Horton's ironic couplets show a compound of attitudes. The democratic origins of the councillors are initially a subject for suspicion: by the end of the extract it is acknowledged that some at least of the 'mushroom men' have nobler motives. Public office is seen primarily as a means of self-advancement: it is only officials who see their first priority as saving on the rates who are found worthy of approval. The 'Joe' who is referred to in the poem is identified in a footnote as Joseph Allday: both Conrad Gill and Asa Briggs, the historians of nineteenth-century Birmingham, identify Allday as the man who, as leader of the 'Economical' party did most to obstruct the progress of local government in the city before its emergence under Joseph Chamberlain in the 1870s as the model of what local administration could achieve.

If Birmingham was suspicious, Liverpool could be unreservedly optimistic about the value to the community of its elected representatives. Hugh Shimmin, editor of the *Liverpool Mercury*, felt that the efforts of the Liverpool town councillors were such as to make them worthy of individual recognition in a handbook in which they were individually identified. His 'Preface' to this work reflects his pride in his city's achievements and status, which he relates directly to the existence of a democratically elected council:

That the town of Liverpool has arrived at a proud station in the commercial world, and that the noble Mersey has become the emporium of the nations is an acknowledged fact. The princes of Tyre in their mercantile splendour have faded away; but the merchant princes of Liverpool are living facts of modern enterprise. Their navy covers the waters of the 'vasty

deep'; their palatial residences in the environs, and
the many magnificent edifices of the town, and its
numerous useful institutions, are all indicative of the
place. Now, to what origin or source can all this be
traced but to the collective wisdom of an assembly
popularly constituted? – an assembly who represent
the people; an elective and elected body, reciprocally
responsible for the common weal.

It is a noticeable feature in the general management
of municipal rule, that the proud position of Liverpool
has triumphed in its elective government, and that
collective wisdom is always to be found in the majority
of an assembly so constituted as the Liverpool town
council.

[Hugh Shimmin], *Pen and Ink Sketches of
Liverpool Town Councillors* (1866), p.viii.

Shimmin's enthusiasm perhaps overcomes his sense of
history – Liverpool's greatness at mid-century could hardly
be attributed solely to a system of government then only
twenty years old. But there can be no denying the confidence
with which he asserts the claims of civic dignity:

It may be presumed that the mayoralty is an object
of laudable ambition to members of the Council. And
it is indeed a splendid achievement. To be the first
man in and the recognised head of the largest sea-port
in the world, whose revenues exceed that of many
independent states; to have a large sum placed at his
disposal to entertain distinguished strangers and his
own townsmen; to have a splendid equipage and body
servants at his command, and the use of a mansion in
which to entertain his guests, unsurpassed for extent
and magnificence – this is a prize worth contending
for, a reward for diligence and ability: and it is open
to all in the race of municipal competition. Many of
its occupants have been men of humble origin, and
who have had to struggle against difficulties, but whose
perseverance, moral worth, and industry enabled

them to surmount all obstacles; and their fellow
townsmen, recognising their qualities, placed them in
the Council; and thus they became chief magistrates
of this vast community.

op. cit., p.4.

Like Horton in Birmingham, Shimmin testifies to the opportunities offered by the elective process to men of humble
origins but he, at least, has no misgivings about the activities
of his elected representatives.

Holders of civic office might aspire to the trappings of
public dignity, but the work that municipal government was
concerned with was of the most basic and practical kind. The
streets of the cities need to be paved, swept and lit – Asa
Briggs notes that for Cardinal Newman gas-lighting was the
touchstone of material progress. Water supplies had to be
regulated, and decent drainage and sewage facilities provided.
Progress was inevitably piecemeal. In many cases local
government was in conflict with vested interest. The interests
of those who paid the rates did not always coincide with
the wider needs of the community. Much depended upon
legislation initiated locally and enacted through private Acts
of Parliament. In the case of Liverpool, for example, the
Liverpool Sanitary Act of 1846 gave to the local council
powers to take responsibility for sewerage, to inspect lodging-
houses, to provide a water-supply and to control industrial
pollution by making factories responsible for the consumption
of their own smoke. The Act also provided for the appointment of a medical officer of health: the council responded
by appointing the distinguished physician William Henry
Duncan, whose enquiries had already shown the extent of
the city's public health problems, and who, once appointed,
worked tirelessly for the improvement of living conditions in
his city. An interesting insight into the functioning of local
administration at literally street-level is given in a footnote to
the English translation of Leon Faucher's *Manchester in 1844*.
Faucher, a French commentator, whose book is remarkably
informative on a number of aspects of Manchester life,
claims that the class-divisions in the city are reflected in the

arrangements for sweeping the streets:

> The authorities of Manchester devote annually
> £5,000 to the cleansing of the town. This sum is
> insufficient, and the organisation essentially defective.
> The first-class streets are cleansed once per week; those
> of the second class, once per fortnight; and the streets
> of the third-class once a month. As to the courts,
> alleys and yards, inhabited by the poorer classes, no
> means are used to ensure their periodical cleansing.
>
> Leon Faucher, *Manchester in 1844; Its Present
> Condition and Future Prospects* (1844, reprinted
> 1969) p.69.

Faucher's translator, 'A Member of the Manchester
Athenaeum', goes into some detail to defend his city against
the charge:

> Formerly, the scavenging department for
> Manchester . . . comprised thirty men in summer, and
> forty in winter. This force was afterwards increased to
> sixty men throughout the year. They swept sixty-five
> streets and places twice per week, sixty-one weekly,
> and four hundred and fifty at periods varying from a
> fortnight to a month. But, during the present year the
> *scavenging-machine cart* has superseded the employ-
> ment of men, in sweeping the streets . . .
> The street-cleaning Company use this machine, and
> have contracted to keep the streets as clean as they
> were before. They stated that they should sweep the
> streets twice as often, and for five hundred pounds
> less, than the expense originally incurred; and the
> result has been a great improvement in the cleanliness
> of the town. All streets in the township, paved or
> unpaved, are to be swept when they require it . . .
> The repair of the surface of all streets devolves upon
> [the Surveyors of Highways]; but the care of the sewers
> belongs to the Council of the Corporation. The
> number of streets, small back streets, courts, and places

> still unpaved, are perhaps five hundred in number, and
> the sewering and repairs of these still rests with
> the owners; but they are amenable to the police
> regulations, as regards nuisances, encroachments,
> obstructions &c., and are lighted and watched at the
> public expense.
>
> op. cit., pp.70–1, n.1.

The details here indicate both the complexity of the difficulties
faced by local authorities and the resourcefulness with which
they approached them. Progress was inevitably slow and
haphazard: the extent to which these developments made an
impact on the most serious problems of the cities remains
open to question but a beginning had been made. From such
beginnings was to emerge an ethos that was to express itself
eventually in the provision of public amenities like wash
houses, baths, parks and libraries, and ultimately in town
planning on a major scale.

Policing, Crime and Public Order

As we have seen, the agglomeration of large numbers of a
new working class in the urban communities provoked anxiety
both locally and nationally about the maintenance of public
order. The system of policing and of local justice that prevailed
at the beginning of the nineteenth century had scarcely been
altered for centuries: it relied primarily upon the authority
of local magistrates and the deployment of parish constables.
Where public order was seriously threatened, the military
were at the behest of the local magistracy. Samuel Bamford,
arrested in 1817 for taking part in banned meetings in
Lancashire, was first taken by 'the deputy-constable' and
'about six or eight police officers, all well armed with staves,
pistols and blunderbusses', before being handed over to a
detachment of dragoons:

> The soldiers were regaled with bread, cheese and ale.
> The street was filled with a great concourse of people,

and some of the military kept guard while the others refreshed . . .

'Captain,' I said, addressing the officer of dragoons, 'are your prisoners to remain without food?'

'Oh, certainly not,' he replied, 'Come up and take what you choose.' George and I, then advanced, and each got a decent wedge of cheese with bread to it, and a quart of ale was also set before us.

Samuel Bamford, *Passages in the Life of a Radical* (1884), Ch. 13.

Such casual civilities scarcely reflect the danger that the arrested men were in, and they were hardly in evidence at Peterloo, where Bamford was arrested for a second time. The widespread political unrest of the first two decades of the nineteenth century, together with the sense that the conurbations were in themselves creating new dimensions of crime led to a movement to establish policing systems relevant to an urban society. The process was a protracted one: however urgent the need for systematic policing might seem, it was countered by anxieties about the powers that might be assumed by a full-time force. The Police Act of 1829 established the Metropolitan force in London, and both the Municipal Corporations Act of 1835 and the County Police Act of 1839 provided for more regular arrangements in the provinces. It was not until 1856, however, that the County and Borough Police Act made the recruitment of full-time salaried forces obligatory throughout the country.

There were two priorities for the maintenance of public order in the cities. On the one hand, policing had to concern itself with local crime; on the other, it was involved, notably during the period of Chartist unrest, with the political dimensions of public order. Where local crime was concerned, a major problem was the development within the cities of criminal ghettoes, areas where the guardians of law and order could scarcely penetrate. The most famous fictional example of this phenomenon is, of course, Jacob's Island in *Oliver Twist*, and in his novel Dickens exposes not only crimes of theft and violence but also the related features of drunkenness and prostitution. *Oliver Twist* has a London setting, but areas similar to Jacob's Island were likely to have existed in any large city. A Victorian writer on the subject of crime, Frederic Hill, gives an account of his experiences in Glasgow in 1837, the date, as it happens, when Dickens began *Oliver Twist*. It replicates the circumstances of the novel quite strikingly:

> I was requested by the Magistrates of Gorbals to inspect a district which they informed me abounded at the same time in poverty, disease, and crime. The greater part of the district is not in Gorbals itself, but is almost close to it, a bridge across the Clyde connecting the two. This portion of the district, which I afterwards learned from Captain Miller, the superintendent of police, is quite the worst in Glasgow, is a compact mass of building intersected only by narrow wynds. It is bounded on the north by the Trongate, on the east by King-street, on the south by the Bridegate, and on the west by Stockwell-street . . .
>
> On descending the stairs of one of the old frail tenements that we examined, I was told that the place is known by the significant name of *Flea Hall*. Most of the shops in these wynds, Captain Miller informed me, are kept by receivers of stolen goods. The inhabitants of one of the wynds, indeed, have so bad a character, that Captain Miller finds it necessary to keep a police-officer constantly stationed in it. Our progress through this abode of crime, of course, made a commotion among the occupants, and we had soon a crowd of attendants, among whom Captain Miller and Mr Brebner recognised many who were but too well known to them. In some instances there was a hesitation about admitting us, but the, to them, familiar cry of *Police!* was instantly followed by the turning of the lock and opening of the door. In one place, we found a party of house-breakers, among whom was the notorious —, who, however, has, I believe, hitherto always contrived to escape conviction; arising in part, no doubt, from the strictness of the Scottish law in always requiring two witnesses. Captain Miller showed

me a room in another house in which a murder had
been committed about a fortnight before. 'He arrived
at the spot,' he said, 'very soon after the deed had
been perpetrated, and found the body of the murdered
woman still warm, and lying across the bedstead. In
the same room, in one corner of the floor, were two
girls, seventeen or eighteen years old, who did not seem
to have been sufficiently roused by the circumstances of
the murder to quit their bed!'

> Frederic Hill, *Crime: Its Amount, Causes, and
> Remedies* (1853), pp.382–3.

Hill describes here a compound of criminal activities, ranging
from the most violent to the petty. At one level local crime
involved murder and serious theft, at another vagrancy and
prostitution. Where the latter is concerned, William Acton,
the Victorian writer on prostitution, related its development
specifically to factors consequent upon urbanisation: 'I regard
prostitution as an inevitable attendant upon civilized, and
especially close-packed, population.' (William Acton, *Prostitution*, 1857; reprinted, ed. Peter Fryer, 1968, p.32.) The forces
that had to contend with criminal activity in the towns and
cities were often of a very rudimentary kind. Since the time
of Shakespeare the village constable had been a figure of fun:
translation to an urban environment seems to have done little
for his dignity. The autobiography of James Hopkinson, a
cabinet-maker who was brought up in Nottingham gives an
account of policing there in the 1830s (Hopkinson's spelling
and punctuation):

> You must know there were no police then as there are
> now and instead of calling the constables bobbies as
> they do now, they were called charleys. It was the
> duty of these charleys to protect the town in the night
> time. Each constable had a district of his own to attend
> to. They were not put on a fresh beat as they are now.
> In different parts of the town watch boxes were placed,
> they were made of wood in form something like a
> Sentinels box about 6 feet 6 in high. It had a seat inside

and room for a man to sit down and make himself comfortable. All well to do people were expected to pay a small sum weekly to support him, as he had to sleep in the day time. He was armed with a constables staff, a rattle and a large lantern. Every half hour he was expected to go his own particular round shouting the time of night or morning as the case might be. And also stating if it was wet or fine or a cloudy morn.

In consequence of having to shout all night there were a many robberies, as the thieves allways knew where the watchman was. They would also occasionally fall asleep in their comfortable watch boxes and forget to go their rounds. Sometimes several men for a lark would push the box over and charley in it with the door downwards so that he could not get out. A very curious incident occur'd to one charley who was a very little man. One night a big stout fellow met him and being merry and inclined for a bit of fun, he took him up in his arms and ran off with him, upon which Mr. Charley shouted at the top of his voice, if you dont put me down I will take you up. And for a long time after it became a bye word in the town If you don't put me down I will take you up.

The Memoirs of James Hopkinson, 1819–1894,
ed. Jocelyn Baty Goodman (1968), pp.13–14.

The legislation of the 1830s undoubtedly made for some improvement in these primitive arrangements. The Municipal Corporations Act, while it did not require the appointment of full-time police, provided for the appointment of watch committees empowered to appoint and swear in constables, an arrangement potentially more systematic than the previous exclusive exercise of magisterial authority. The County Police Act of 1839 was a direct response to the threat posed by Chartism, but it provided for a further extension of police powers generally. The evidence suggests that outside London it was the larger cities like Manchester, Liverpool and Birmingham that were the most densely policed. A report of

1847 by Captain Willis, Chief Constable of Manchester, quoted by Hill, seems remarkably sanguine in its account of a general improvement in law and order in the city:

'I have been superintendent of police at Manchester about five years and a half. During that time there has been a considerable decrease in crime, and a marked general improvement in the orderly conduct of the population . . . The offences committed at present are of a less serious character than they were five years ago. There are fewer robberies with violence than formerly; indeed, such an offence is now of rare occurrence, and, when committed, it generally appears that the party robbed was drunk at the time, and in the company of women of the town . . . The conduct of the working classes of Manchester since trade became bad, and commercial distress prevailed, has been highly praiseworthy. Though there has been much suffering, there has been no violence; and except that there have been more petty thefts than usual, there has been no increase of crime of any kind. These thefts have been committed chiefly by persons who, even when trade is good, gain their livelihood, in part, at least, by stealing. Such persons, when trade becomes bad, are, of course, the first to be dismissed from the factories, and then they depend wholly on stealing. Since trade has somewhat improved, and the number out of employment has also diminished . . . The great mass of the offenders belong to the most ignorant part of the population, whether English or Irish. Of more than six thousand persons apprehended last year, less than twenty had received a superior education to mere reading and writing. I attribute the absence of violence of late, on the part of the working classes, and the comparative rarity of strikes, very much to the greater spread of intelligence among them. I think that many of them are now convinced that such conduct only adds to their suffering, and injures themselves even more than it injures their employers.'

Hill, op. cit., pp.30–1.

Hill quotes a second report from Willis, dated 1849, which repeats the optimism of his observations here. A Chief Constable would, of course, have his own reasons for advertising the effectiveness of his force, but it is interesting to see here the extent to which he is prepared to relate the incidence of crime to larger social factors like the trade cycle, unemployment and education. Hill himself was an optimist about the social dimensions of criminality, believing, like many of his contemporaries, that the causes of crime could be, in his term, 'remedied', notably by educating the young in their social and moral obligations, and he adduces Willis's reports as evidence of what can be achieved 'even under the present very imperfect arrangements', and to 'encourage the hope that by well-considered and well-directed exertions the whole amount of crime in this country may be greatly reduced and softened in character as no longer to affect, in a material degree, the general happiness of society.' (op. cit, p.32).

As the reports quoted by Hill show, anxiety about the political dimensions of public order invariably colours the more general discussion of the issue at this time. The distinction between what we have referred to as 'local' crime and political crime was not always a simple one: crimes against property and against the person might well have a political dimension, as in the murder of Thomas Ashton, a Lancashire mill-owner's son, in 1831. The murderers were purportedly in the pay of local trades unionists and, while she herself denied making direct reference to it, it is likely that memory of the crime lies behind Mrs Gaskell's fictionalisation of a murder in the union cause in *Mary Barton*. As late as 1866 the Sheffield outrages, a series of violent acts by workers determined to maintain union solidarity, were the basis of a novel by Charles Reade in which the hero, a newcomer to Sheffield, is attacked for refusing to accede to the union's demands. His belief that the police might protect him is dismissed by one of his Sheffield friends, who advises him to take his own measures of self-defence:

'Thank you sir!' said Harry, warmly, 'But ought not the police to afford me protection outside?'

'The police! You might as well go to the beadle.
No; change your lodging, if you think they know it.
Don't let them track you home. Buy a brace of pistols,
and, if they catch you in a dark place, and try to do
you, give them a barrel or two before they can strike
a blow. Not one of *them* will ever tell the police, not
if you shot his own brother dead at that game. The
law is a dead letter here, sir. You've nothing to expect
from it, and nothing to fear.'

'Good heavens! Am I in England?'

'In England? No. You are in Hillsborough.'

> Charles Reade, *Put Yourself in His Place* (1866),
> Ch. 5.

Fear of the trade unions undoubtedly led commentators to
exaggerate their reputation for violence, and when this finds
expression in fiction the element of melodrama is rarely
absent. The Ashton murder achieved the status of myth at
least in part because it was an isolated and thus notorious
event: the unions themselves, as in the Sheffield instance,
invariably repudiated violence of this kind. But the myth
itself was strong enough to be believed, and in the context of
the political climate of the 1830s and 40s at least it is not
difficult to see why that should have been the case.

In the decade immediately following the first Reform Bill,
no less than in the years leading up to Peterloo, it was thought
necessary to keep the militia at readiness to deal with political
unrest. The specific aim of Chartism was to achieve political
reform: its growth as an expression of working-class grievance
was fuelled by the realities of economic hardship and by the
consequences of reforms like the New Poor Law of 1834,
expressly designed as an instrument of social control, combi-
ning efficiency of organisation with an explicitly deterrent
intention. As the movement grew, working people met in
large crowds on open spaces near the great cities to listen to
their orators, and to demonstrate their solidarity; the effect
on the authorities was inevitably frightening in the extreme.
Retrospectively it is possible to say that the actual incidence

of violence committed was remarkably limited, but in newspapers like Fergus O'Connor's *Northern Star*, published from Leeds, the rhetoric of revolution was a commonplace. Reporting a speech made to a Chartist gathering in Birmingham in 1838 by the moderate leader, Thomas Attwood, for example, it commented:

> Hear one sentence from Mr Attwood's address, 'The men of Birmingham,' he said, 'were willing either to assist or lead them on (Cheers) in the cause of peace, loyalty, and order. The men of Birmingham would not shrink from assisting them even to the *Death*.' Let that sentiment be engraven upon the heart of every white slave, and let him in his bondage, hug his chains, and wear the fetters he had forged for himself, if one general response of co-operation with the good men of Birmingham does not proclaim universal liberty . . . 'Even to the Death.' How marvellously does this sentiment accord with those expressed in the objects of The Great Northern Union, 'to use physical force if necessary.' Moral power is a shadow. Physical force is the substance.
>
> *The Northern Star*, 2 June 1838.

The Chartist movement was divided between those who were prepared to threaten violence, and those who rejected it; inevitably it was the former party who made the most impact. Handbills of the time were categoric in their incitement to violence and if, with the advantage of hindsight, we can see that the emotive impact of such incitements outweighed their practical effectiveness, it can hardly have looked like that at the time. The embryonic police forces were not expected to cope with the dangers embodied in such threats, and in the late 1830s, as in the early years of the century, the militia were deployed throughout the country to counter the possibility of insurrection as and where it occurred.

The Chartist movement came to its climax in 1839 with the events leading up to the presentation of the People's Charter to Parliament. After considerable delay the first Chartist

1. 'Manchester', from George Catt, *The Pictorial History of Manchester*, 1843. As in similar views of Manchester of this period, the mill chimneys and towers and spires of the industrial city are seen from an idealised rural viewpoint.

MANCHESTER, GETTING UP THE STEAM.

2. 'Manchester, Getting up the Steam', from *The Builder*, 1853.

3. Rodney Street, Liverpool. Built in the first decade of the nineteenth century, this elegant street was to house prominent figures amongst Liverpool's business and professional communities. W.E. Gladstone was born in 1809 in the house shown.

4. Birmingham: a Working-Class Court. A photograph taken in the early 1870s, and reflecting living conditions common in the city at mid-century.

5. Policemen in Manchester, c.1850–60. The uniforms and order of drill reflect the organisation and authority of the new city police forces.

6. Leeds Town Hall in 1858, the year of its opening. The grandeur and scale of the building are a testimony to Victorian civic pride.

Convention was transferred from London to Birmingham. Unlike the metropolis, Birmingham had as yet no full-scale police force. A major figure in the Convention was William Lovett. In his autobiography he describes what have become known as the Bull Ring riots, when the civic authorities, feeling themselves unable to cope with the threat of disturbance, and reluctant to summon the militia, called for police reinforcements from London to disperse a banned meeting. The moment was a crucial one for the policing of the urban communities, for it became the pretext for the County Police Act of 1839 which, while its measures were only of limited effect, established the principle that the provincial regions, like London, should have their own effective police forces:

> The following are the circumstances that led to my arrest, and that of my fellow-prisoner, Mr Collins: – It appears that the middle classes of Birmingham, during the agitation for *the Reform Bill*, were in the habit of meeting in the Bull-ring, in conjunction with the working classes, during a portion of their dinner hours and in the evenings, for the purpose of hearing the news of the day; when stirring appeals from the newspapers were read, and speeches made regarding the measure then before Parliament. The Reform Bill, however, being passed, a great change was soon seen in the political conduct of some of the leading reformers of Birmingham, as well as of other towns. *Municipal reform* had given power and authority to some, and Whig patronage snug places to others. When, however, the agitation for the People's Charter commenced, the working classes, following the example of their former leaders, began to hold their meetings also in the Bull-ring. But this of course was not to be endured by the ex-reform authorities; what was once right and legal in themselves was denounced as seditious and treasonable in the multitude. The poor infatuated workers, however, could not perceive the distinction of the Birmingham authorities between the two political measures, but continued to meet as usual; and though several of them were arrested, and held to bail for their

obtuseness, their meetings were kept up. At last the governing powers of Birmingham, indignant at such proceedings, sent up to London to their former friends and allies requesting them to send down a strong posse of the new police to assist them. They came down by rail, and were no sooner out of their vans than they were led on by the authorities, truncheon in hand, and commenced a furious onslaught upon the men, women, and children who were assembled in the Bull-ring listening peaceably to a person reading the newspaper.

The Life and Struggles of William Lovett (1876, reprinted with a Preface by R. H. Tawney 1967), pp. 179–80.

Chartism was the last expression of political unrest on a national scale in Britain in the nineteenth century. Increasingly the police forces brought into being by the 1856 County and Borough Police Act had to deal with local crime. The political function remained, however: in his memoirs the Manchester police superintendent James Bent records how, as late as 1881, he and six other officers were issued with cutlasses when sent to the site of a colliery strike. (James Bent, *Criminal Life: Reminiscences of Forty-Two Years as a Police Officer*, 1891, p. 25.) When new police stations were built, they usually featured a pair of riot doors, installed just inside the entrances to defend against incursion. Urban policing in the later part of the century was inevitably a brutal business: an officer making an arrest, for example, had the problem of getting his prisoner back to the station without the aid of transport, and often in the face of a hostile crowd. The public image of the police was ambivalent, as is reflected by the traditions of music hall and of popular fiction and journalism. Music hall, which, as it happens, developed concurrently with the emergence of the police forces, was cynical about police integrity. In his autobiography Sir Robert Mark points out that the famous song of the 1880s 'If you want to know the time, ask a policeman' embodies the central irony that the police were reputed to come by their watches by stealing them from drunks: the joke was one that went back to the beginning of the force. (Sir Robert Mark, *In the Office of Constable*, 1978, p.17.) On the other hand, fictional detectives like Dickens's Inspector Bucket in *Bleak House* and Wilkie Collins's Sergeant Cuff in *The Moonstone* (1868) were accredited with near superhuman powers. Police work exercised a considerable attraction over the popular imagination: a common form of journalistic enquiry was the article based on a visit to criminal dens in the company of a police officer. In a pamphlet written in the late 1860s, the Manchester journalist Junius Junior describes a nocturnal visit to cheap lodging-houses in the city:

> How complete the power of the police! Go where we will . . . the fact is not to be denied. 'Sit up! come! turn your face this way!' and, nine cases out of ten, the man or woman or child instantly obeys, passive as a lamb. Sternness, and a habit of speaking with decision, have rendered these lodgers submissive to a degree which is perfectly astonishing. The arm of the law has bent their strong and obstinate wills. The consciousness that they are constantly outraging the law, and are correspondingly amenable to it, is the source of their obedience. For the law, in the records of the police, holds their biographies in its iron grasp; not a detected crime of the past or present which cannot be revealed and which has not its withering application to the criminal's future.
>
> Junius Junior, *Life in the Low Parts of Manchester: A Midnight Visit to the Thieves and Common Lodging Houses About the City*, n.d. [1869].

Junior's reference to police records suggests the beginnings of modern policing, but its testimony to the power of the police and to the criminals' respect for it, one suspects, must contain elements of fantasy. The memoirs of serving policemen like Bent and his detective contemporary, Jerome Caminada, who also served in the Manchester force at this time, record the pride of professional policemen, but at the same time they show the hazards of the job. Describing his experiences as a young policeman on the beat in the late 1860s Caminada tells of his attempts to quell a domestic affray:

> Now was the time to show my authority, and I at once gave them to understand, in no uncertain terms, that if there was any more disturbance, I should lock them up. But I soon found that whatever opinion I had of my own importance, neither the uniform nor the 'little brief authority' of the newly-made policeman had any terror for these fiends. I was soon besieged with questions – 'Who sent for thee?' 'What art tha doin' here?' 'Canner we have a row in ar' own house, wi'out thee interfering?' and so on. But as in the policeman's uniform they evidently thought they saw a common enemy, the two brothers made up their quarrel, and were joined by the rest of the family, and as the five allies made common cause not only in resenting my interference and setting my authority at defiance, but were inclined 'to go for the bobby,' I began to see that there was a likelihood of being put under the sofa myself; so thinking, under the circumstances, that discretion was the better part of valour, I backed out into the street, threatening at the same time what would be the consequences if I heard any more noise. I might have saved my breath, for the door was immediately slammed in my face, and having got rid of the common enemy, the alliance was at once broken up, the allies turned on each other again, and the fight and disturbance was carried on until the early hours of the morning. Then followed a silence which told that they had fallen asleep from sheer exhaustion.
>
> Jerome Caminada, *Twenty-Five Years of Detective Life* (1901), Vol. II, pp.31–2.

Caminada joined the Manchester city police in 1868 and rose to the rank of superintendent by his retirement in 1899. This is one of the milder of his experiences, and while his autobiography records some astonishing feats of self-preservation, together with his successes as a detective, he acknowledges in his final pages that the effect of the urban police can never be more than partial. 'By the sedate ratepayer and orderly citizen', he says, the policeman 'is looked upon with satisfaction as the man who has joint charge of his interests, and is ready to help in the event of any emergency or unlawful interruption.' Nevertheless, 'the most perfect police system that human ingenuity can devise will never provide against a certain percentage of undetected crime in any community.'

(op. cit., pp.501, 511–2.)

Religion

Overt agencies of social control in the cities were supported by other cultural institutions, notably those of religion and education. In the case of religion, parochial and chapel systems which had been inherited from the rural past were to prove inadequate to the demands of the new urban culture; from the early years of the nineteenth century concern was expressed by the churches about their ineffectiveness in densely populated areas. The impulse of Evangelicalism, the dominant development both within and beyond the established church in the early nineteenth century, was towards missionary endeavour: the need for such activity was seen to be as imperative at home as it was abroad. The 1851 census added an investigation of religious practice to its more general enquiries. The answers confirmed what had been suspected. Throughout the country there were over five million absentees from church on the day the census was taken. Within the industrial cities the level of absence was higher than elsewhere: it was thus clear that the churches were largely failing to reach the urban working class. The organiser of the census, Horace Mann, identified these issues precisely in his report:

> The most important fact which this investigation as to attendance brings before us is, unquestionably, the alarming number of the non-attendants. Even in the least unfavourable aspect of the figures just presented, and assuming (as no doubt is right) that the 5,288,294

absent every Sunday are not always the same individuals, it must be apparent that a sadly formidable portion of the English people are habitual neglecters of the public ordinances of religion. Nor is it difficult to indicate to what particular class of the community this portion in the main belongs. The middle classes have augmented rather than diminished that devotional sentiment and strictness of attention to religious services by which, for several centuries, they have been so eminently distinguished. With the upper classes, too, the subject of religion has obtained of late a marked degree of notice, and a regular church-attendance is now ranked amongst the regular proprieties of life. It is to satisfy the wants of these two classes that the number of religious structures has of late years so increased. But while the *labouring* myriads of our country have been multiplying with our multiplied material prosperity, it cannot, it is feared, be stated that a corresponding increase has occurred in the attendance of this class in our religious edifices. More especially in cities and large towns it is observable how absolutely insignificant a portion of the congregations is composed of artisans.

> H. Mann, *Census of Religious Worship* (1851),
> reprinted in R. P. Flindall, ed., *The Church of
> England, 1815–1948* (1972), p.133.

The methodology of the 1851 census has been challenged by both contemporary and modern commentators, but it is difficult to deny the central premises of Mann's report. According to Edward Miall, the editor of *The Nonconformist*, writing just before the census was taken:

There lies at the bottom of society in this country, and especially in the metropolis and the more populous town, a thick sediment of physical destitution, which it is morally impossible for the light of Christianity to penetrate and purify.

> Edward Miall, *The British Churches in Relation
> to the British People* (1849), p.348.

Miall continues, 'What can Christianity do with this terrific mass of rottenness?' and would seem to suggest that there can be no answer to his rhetorical question. There is an element of realism in his pessimism, for whatever claims may be made for evangelical activity in the cities, it is doubtful whether its ministrations substantially affected those living at the lowest levels of society. Miall's contemporaries, however, were not prepared to give up so easily, and from the early years of the nineteenth century organisations for the religious improvement of the urban poor proliferated. The tract fiction published by bodies like the Society for the Promotion of Christian Knowledge and the Religious Tract Society was one attempt to spread the Christian message. In perhaps the most famous of these stories, Hesba Stretton's *Jessica's First Prayer*, the heroine, a ragged child, finds herself in a church for the first time, where she is told by the verger that the church 'isn't any place for such as you. It's for ladies and gentlemen.' The child continues the conversation:

> 'What do the ladies and gentlemen do when they come here? Tell me, and I'll be off sharp.'
> 'They come to pray,' whispered Daniel.
> 'What is pray?' asked Jessica.
> 'Bless the child!' cried Daniel in perplexity. 'Why, they kneel down in those pews, most of them sit though, and the minister up in the pulpit tells God what they want.'
> Jessica gazed into his face with such an air of bewilderment that a faint smile crept over the sedate face of the pew-opener.
> 'What is a minister and God?' she said; 'and do ladies and gentlemen want anything? I thought they'd everything they wanted.'
>
> Hesba Stretton, *Jessica's First Prayer* (1866),
> Ch. 3.

Like Dickens's Jo in *Bleak House*, Jessica is a representative of the numerous children of the cities who, interrogated by parliamentary commissioners or by journalistic investigators like Henry Mayhew, revealed an absolute ignorance of the most elementary Christian precepts.

The response of the Church of England to the situation in the cities was reflected not only by missionary schemes, but by the reform of its administrative arrangements within the urban communities, and above all by the building of new churches in the towns and cities, financed often by industrial wealth. As the Reverend Hugh James Rose wrote to W. F. Hook, the reforming Vicar of Leeds:

> I have long maintained that if the richer manufacturing laity are taught their duty to the souls of those whose bodies they use as machines for making money, and in consequence . . . they build churches . . . the manufacturing districts may become towers of strength for the Church.
>
> Quoted in W. R. W. Stephens, *The Life and Letters of Walter Farquhar Hook* (1878), Vol. I, p.413.

The foundation of the Church Building Society, together with the Church Building Act of 1818, initiated a wave of church-building which was to last well into the nineteenth century. Hook, soon after his appointment to Leeds in 1837, set about the tasks of rebuilding his church and reforming the administration of his parish. His biographer records the difficulties which faced him: 'The population had risen from 53,162 in 1801 to 123,393 in 1831. The provision on the part of the Church for the spiritual necessities of the place was and had long been miserably inadequate.' (op. cit.) Vol. I, p.371.) Within months of Hook's taking charge, however, 'The congregation . . . became so large that scarcely standing room could be found at the Sunday services. Much space was wasted by the large appropriated pews and galleries with which the church was encumbered. The poor sometimes went an hour before the time of service, yet were unable to get in.' (Vol. I, p.378.) Undeterred, Hook completely rebuilt his church and organised classes and meetings for his parishioners, at one point presenting as many as a thousand of them for confirmation at a single service. By such means he aimed not only to propagate the religious practices of the Established Church, but that version of them – Tractarian as opposed to the broader forms of evangelicalism – to which he himself subscribed. Behind the movement to evangelise lay sectarian considerations which were both a strength and a weakness: a strength in that they intensified the sense of urgency, and a weakness in that they were divisive. When the ecclesiologist A. W. N. Pugin wrote in the conclusion to his *Contrasts* (1836), a study of styles of architecture, that 'as it is, everything glorious about the English churches is Catholic, everything debased and hideous, Protestant', he revealed himself as an ambiguous ally for the expansionist church builders he sought to advise.

For all the efforts of men like Hook the impact of conventional church practices was inevitably limited. As one of his curates wrote, 'had we ten new churches . . . with a corresponding staff of clergy, we should not have one too many.' (Stephens, Vol. I, pp.373–4). More robust attitudes within the Established Church were proposed by Charles Kingsley, who with F. D. Maurice and J. M. Ludlow founded the Christian Socialist movement in the aftermath of the final failure of Chartism. Shortly after the debacle of the 1848 petition to Parliament Kingsley distributed a poster headed WORKMEN OF ENGLAND! which began:

WORKMEN OF ENGLAND! You say that you are wronged. Many of you are wronged; and many besides yourselves know it. Almost all men who have heads and hearts know it – above all the working clergy know it. They go into your houses, they see the shameful filth and darkness in which you are forced to live crowded together; they see your children growing up in ignorance and temptation, for want of fit education; they see intelligent and well-read men among you, shut out from a Freeman's just right of voting; and they see too the noble patience and self-

control with which you have as yet borne these evils.
They see it, and God sees it.

Reprinted in *Charles Kingsley: His Letters and
Memories of His Life, edited by his wife* (2 vols,
1877), Vol. I, p.156.

This was followed up by a new penny journal, *Politics for the
People*, in an early number of which Kingsley confessed, 'We
have used the Bible as if it was a mere special constable's
handbook – an opium-dose for keeping beasts of burden
patient while they were being over-loaded.' (*Politics for the
People*, No. 4, 27 May 1848, p.58.) *Politics for the People*,
however, like Christian Socialism itself as an effective
movement, was short-lived. Kingsley's insistence that the
clergy could and did identify with the sufferings of the poor
was compromised by the fact that his rhetoric was more
powerful than practical, while his journal rejected the idea of
immediate universal suffrage and discouraged working-class
activism. The suspicion was inevitable that Christian Socialism
was basically intended to keep working men in their place.

Where the dissenting churches were concerned, the figures
of the 1851 census appeared to give considerable encouragement, for they revealed that attendance at chapel was close
to parity with attendance at church. Furthermore, in many
of the industrial areas Nonconformity was in the lead. In
Hook's Leeds, for example, nearly 42 per cent of those
attending divine service on the day of the census were
Methodists, as against 32 per cent who were Anglicans, while
in Sheffield the proportions for the same denominations were
36 per cent for the Methodists (of all persuasions) and 34 per
cent for the Established Church. In Sheffield, other dissenting
congregations accounted for a further 19 per cent, and Roman
Catholics and Jews for the remainder. As an index of the
involvement of Nonconformity with Miall's 'terrific mass of
rottenness', however, these figures are deceptive. In the
nineteenth century Dissent – and nowhere more so than
amongst the industrial and commercial classes – was the creed
of the upwardly mobile, distancing itself from the urban
working class by its very success amongst their employers.

Traditionally Dissent had been strong in the provinces and amongst the poorer sections of society. Thomas Cooper, the Chartist, testifies to its formative influence in his autobiography:

> It cannot be supposed that, with a nature so emotional as mine, I had listened to the earnest prayers of my teachers in the Methodist Sunday School, and joined in the singing so delightedly, both in church and chapel, and heard sermons, without having religious impressions. From a child I felt these. Often, during our reading of the gospels, verse by verse, as we stood in class, at the Free school, the Saviour seemed almost visible to me as I read of his deeds of mercy and love. The singing of our morning and evening hymns, and repetition, on our knees, of the Lord's prayer, had always a solemnizing effect on me, and doubtless, seeds of spiritual good were sown thus early in my mind, never to be really destroyed.
>
> Thomas Cooper, *The Life of Thomas Cooper, written by himself* (1872), Ch. 4., p.36.

Cooper is writing of the provincial town of Gainsborough; the period is 1816–1820. The experience he describes is fictionalised in the novels of George Eliot: both writers testify to its significance for them personally, and in terms of the cultural history of the century. But equally significant sources of nineteenth-century Nonconformity were the Quaker and Unitarian business elites which, supported by intermarriage and family networks, came to predominate in cities like Birmingham, Manchester and Liverpool. In Birmingham Quaker families had emerged as a powerful force in business through the eighteenth century: in Cross Street Chapel in Manchester, William Gaskell, husband of the novelist, ministered from 1828 until his death over fifty years later to a Unitarian congregation containing many of the city's business and intellectual leaders. As the nineteenth century saw, in George Eliot's phrase, 'the new prosperity of dissent' (*Felix Holt*, Bk. I, Ch. 4), so, to take the useful distinction of Clyde Binfield, 'Dissent' became 'Nonconformity'. (Clyde Binfield,

*So Down To Prayers: Studies in English Non-Conformity
1790–1920*, 1977, p.12.) In so doing, it developed an inevitable distance from the working-class elements of its origins.
Binfield cites the observations of a contemporary observer of
the phenomenon, looking back from the end of the century:

> There were many congregational and Unitarian Chap-
> els in Manchester and Salford and the smaller Lan-
> cashire towns . . . in which the arrival in the street
> outside of carriages drawn by horseflesh in its most
> mettlesome examples betokened with certainty the
> approaching end of the sermon and was indeed as
> much part of the order of worship as the collection or
> the concluding hymn.
>
> > *Men of the Period: Lancashire* (1895),
> > cit. Binfield, op. cit., p.169.

Given these developments, it is inevitable that the responsibility felt by Nonconformity for the underprivileged should
express itself not in terms of welcoming them into the
corporate body of the church but through visiting and other
explicitly missionary activity. Such activities, often related to
specific issues, like temperance or the rescue of 'fallen women',
are in themselves an expression of social division: the urban
poor are seen, like the heathen, as separate beings in need of
conversion and redemption. All of the religious denominations engaged in mission work, but it was often the preoccupa-
tion of the smaller dissenting sects who had been excluded
from the general tendency towards economic self-advancement. A vivid account of the realities of mission work in the
city slums is given in a Manchester pamphlet of 1870 by
Alfred Alsop, a local lay-preacher:

> On a Saturday evening, during February, we held a
> midnight open-air mission, commencing at eleven
> o'clock, and was continued [sic] till a quarter past
> twelve, and there were specimens of drunkards, of all
> shapes, sizes and ages, of both sexes. The question as
> to whether there will be a fire in hell has often been
> asked; but whether or no, if such beings as those are

to form part of the company of the lower regions, it will, to the moralist, be a sufficient *hell*. Supposing there were no fire, but which the Word of God declares emphatically there is, the sunken degraded state of the people, particularly the young men and women, was, and is, beyond all description. That Saturday evening it seemed as if hell itself had vomited its fiery nature into the heads and hearts of those poor creatures, for they yelled, screamed, and rolled about, waved their arms like so many maniacs; but God was with us, and we have every reason to believe that the word went with power, for since then great good has *been the result* of that mission.

Alfred Alsop, *A Cry for Help from the Slums*,
n.d. [1870], p.10.

Alsop, who described his mission as 'strictly unsectarian', continues, 'Christian men and women, members of churches and chapels, *the city groans* beneath some terrible curse, and that curse is Drink'. The language is melodramatic, but that cannot detract from the reality of what men such as he had to face.

There remain the Roman Catholics. The Emancipation Act of 1829 had freed them from formal constraints, but at that time they were a somewhat ineffectual force; as Cardinal Newman described them looking back from the 1850s, 'a few adherents of the Old religion, moving silently and sorrowfully about . . . a set of poor Irishmen, coming and going at harvest time, or . . . lodged in a miserable quarter of the vast metropolis.' (John Henry Newman, 'The Second Spring', 1852, *Sermons Preached on Various Occasions*, 6th edn, 1887, p.171.) The flood of immigration in the 1840s increased Newman's 'set of poor Irishmen' to a very considerable force, which in principle gave the Catholics a considerable constituency, particularly in the cities. The immigrant communities were desperately impoverished, and tended to keep very much to themselves, and, despite the enthusiasm generated by the Oxford Movement, Catholicism remained very much on the defensive. Faced by the hostility aroused by the restoration of the Catholic hierarchy in 1850, Newman recommended a strategy of containment:

> Let each stand on his own ground; let each approve himself in his own neighbourhood; if each portion is defended, the whole is secured . . . And then if troubled times come on, and the enemy rages, and his many voices go forth from one centre through all England . . . why in that case the Birmingham people will say, "Catholics doubtless are an infamous set, and not to be trusted . . . but somehow an exception must be made for the Catholics of Birmingham. They are not like the rest: they are indeed a shocking set at Manchester, Preston, Blackburn and Liverpool; but however you account for it, they are respectable men here" . . . And in like manner, the Manchester people will say, "Oh, certainly, Popery is horrible, and must be kept down. Still let us give the devil his due, they are a remarkably excellent body of men here, and we will take care no one does them any harm."

> John Henry Newman, *Lectures on the Present Position of Catholics in England* (1852), Fifth edn, pp.386–7.

Newman's advice testifies to the fact that Catholic strength was centred in the towns and cities, but it shows also the extent to which Catholics still saw themselves as a threatened group. Catholic clergy ministered stoically to their far from reliable flock: amongst them was to be the poet Gerard Manley Hopkins who in 1879 in a letter to Robert Bridges recorded his experience of the towns of north west England:

> Leigh is a town smaller and with less dignity than Rochdale and in a flat; the houses red, mean, and two storied; there are a dozen mills or so, and coalpits also; the air is charged with smoke as well as damp; but the people are hearty . . . I was yesterday at St. Helen's, probably the most repulsive place in Lancashire or out of the black country. The stench of

sulphuretted hydrogen rolls in the air and films of the same gas form on railing and pavement.

> Gerard Manley Hopkins, *Selected Prose*, ed.
> Gerald Roberts (1980), pp.80–1.

In such surroundings Hopkins inevitably became dispirited: in one of his sermons he dwelt upon the vices of the urban poor: 'Now more than ever is there riotous company, drunkenness, lewdness, strife, brawling, even bloodshed. From Liverpool he wrote, 'I remarked for the thousandth time with sorrow and loathing the base and bespotted features of the Liverpool crowd . . . I am told Sheffield is worse though.' (*Selected Prose*, p.87, p.97.) Hopkins's experience had told him that the Catholic Church, like the other denominations, could do little to christianise the urban poor.

Education

Churches of all denominations saw the provision of education as one of their functions. Throughout the period under our consideration they were amongst the main providers of education for working-class children, through Sunday schools and through the schools of the two educational societies, the National Society (Anglican) and the British and Foreign Schools Society (Nonconformist). The problem of school provision in urban areas paralleled that of providing places for worship. It was most difficult in those areas where the need appeared to be greatest. This point was made by the Rev. J. S. Howson in a paper given to the congress of the National Association for the Promotion of Social Science held in Liverpool in 1859.

> All the facilities are found in one class of districts –
> large church and chapel collections, local proximity of
> the wealthy, manageable numbers of the poor: all the
> difficulties in another class of districts – crowded
> population, poverty, degradation, and absolute re-

moval from the presence, and therefore the sympathy of the rich.

J. S. Howson, 'Report on Popular Education in
Liverpool', *Transactions of the National
Association for the Promotion of Social Science*
(1859), p.423.

The system of Privy Council grants for education which required that they should be matched by local subscriptions reinforced this disparity so that, as Howson said, 'there is a tendency in the system to give help to those who need little help, and to pass by those who need it most.' (Ibid.)

It was partly the failure of this 'voluntary' system to provide for the most deprived children who then, like Jessica (see p.91), grew up in total ignorance of religion, which led many to support the setting up of a compulsory national system of education. This reaction is anticipated by Wordsworth in a passage in his long reflective poem, *The Excursion*:

> O for the coming of that glorious time
> When, prizing knowledge as her noblest wealth
> And best protection, this Imperial Realm,
> While she exacts allegiance, shall admit,
> An obligation, on her part, to *teach*
> Them who are born to serve her and obey;
> Binding herself by statute to secure
> For all the children whom her soil maintains
> The rudiments of letters, and inform
> The mind with moral and religious truth,
> Both understood and practised, – so that none,
> However destitute, be left to droop
> By culture unsustained; or run
> Into a wild disorder; or be forced
> To drudge through a weary life without the help
> Of intellectual implements and tools;
> A savage horde among the civilised,
> A servile band among the lordly free!

William Wordsworth, *The Excursion* (1814),
Bk. IX,ll.293–310.

Wordsworth foresees education bringing advantages to society as well as the individual, in that it will provide protection for the community from the uneducated who have the potential to become 'a savage horde' and run into 'a wild disorder'. This concern for social order and social control is apparent in the speeches and writings of many who advocated the extension of working-class education, particularly in the urban areas.

Lord Ashley (later Earl of Shaftesbury) addressed himself to this problem in a speech to the House of Commons in 1843. He argued strongly in favour of 'diffusing the benefits of a moral and religious education among the working class' in order that the 'displacement of the whole system of society' could be avoided. His evidence for the existence of a serious problem is all drawn from the manufacturing towns, large and small. In the following extract, relating to Birmingham, he identifies the crime and delinquency of the urban areas with the inadequacy of their educational provision and contrasts the number of schools (669) with the number of places 'for the practice of vice' (998).

I will next take the town of Birmingham; and it will be seen by the police returns for 1841, that the number of persons who were taken into custody was 5,556, of these the males were 4,537, and the females 1,018. Of these there could neither read nor write, 2,711; who could read only and write imperfectly, 2,504; read and write well, 206; having superior instruction, 36. . . . Now from a report on the state of education in the town of Birmingham, made by the Birmingham Statistical Society . . . I find that the total number of schools of all kinds in the town of Birmingham is 669; but then the society calls everything a school where a child receives any sort of instruction, perhaps in a place more fitted to be a sty or coal-hole. Now out of the whole mass of the entire population of Birmingham there were 27,659 scholars. A vast proportion of these schools are what are called 'dame schools'; and what these are in truth, may be known by the surveyors report, who says of them, 'moral and religious instruction forms no part of the system in dame-schools. A mistress in one of this class of schools on being asked whether she gave moral instruction to her scholars, replied, "No, I can't afford it at 3d. a-week." Several did not know the meaning of the question. Very few appeared to think it was a part of their duty.'

Hansard, Vol. LXVII (28 February to 24 March 1843), pp.51–3.

After reinforcing his argument with a detailed breakdown of the number of criminal haunts in the city, Ashley concludes with a reference to what he saw as the specific needs of girls in this context:

I will close . . . by reading to the House an extract from a report, made by a committee of medical gentlemen in Birmingham, who, in the most benevolent spirit, devoted themselves to an examination of the state of Birmingham; and who, looking to the removal of the growing evils that threatens the population, assert, that –

'The first and most prominent suggestion is, the better education of the females in the arts of domestic economy. To the extreme ignorance of domestic management, on the part of the wives of the mechanics, is much of the misery and want of comfort to be traced. Numerous instances have occurred to us of the confirmed drunkard who attributes his habits of dissipation to a wretched home.'

Ibid.

The medical gentlemen may have been somewhat naive in their acceptance of the drunkard's explanation, but concern about the need to educate working-class girls in the domestic arts was frequently expressed at this time. Girls who worked from an early age or whose mothers worked had little opportunity to learn at home, as Mrs Gaskell's Mrs Wilson explains to Mary Barton:

'If you'll believe me, Mary, there never was such a born goose at house-keeping as I were; and yet he married me! I had been in a factory sin' five years old a'most, and I knew nought about cleaning, or cooking, let alone washing or such like work. The day after we were married, he went to his work at after breakfast, and says he, "Jenny, we'll have the cold beef, and potatoes, and that's a dinner for a prince." I were anxious to make him comfortable, God knows how anxious. And yet I'd no notion how to cook a potato. I know'd they were boiled, and know'd their skins were taken off, and that were all.'

Mary Barton, Ch. 10.

Ashley's more general remarks about the moral state of the manufacturing districts did not go unchallenged. In the second of two open letters to Sir Robert Peel, Edward Baines, the editor of the *Leeds Mercury* and a strong supporter of the voluntary principle in education, defended both the manufacturing districts and their religious and educational provision:

You are aware, Sir, that the prejudice against the Manufacturing Districts is of much older date than Lord Ashley's speech or the Report of the Children's Employment Commissioners. It has respect not merely to the alleged want of education and religious instruction, but to the social conditions of the people and the nature and effects of their employments. This prejudice . . . has been industriously cultivated by many persons, and from various motives . . . I fear it may be said that in the South of England there is a general impression that the Manufacturing Districts are scenes of vice, ignorance, sedition, irreligion, cruelty and wretchedness, – that in all these things they are believed to have a bad pre-eminence over the rural population, and the cities and towns which are not seats of manufactures, – that they are even looked upon with lively alarm, under the impression that their moral condition is daily growing worse.

Edward Baines, 'Letter to the Right Hon. Sir Robert Peel, June 24, 1843', reprinted in *The Factory Education Bill of 1843: Six Pamphlets*, New York (1972), Part 6, p.53.

Baines saw Ashley's attack on the inadequacy of educational provision in the factory towns as part of a wider struggle between the landed interest and the manufacturing interest, between the rural and the urban. In his first letter to Peel (16 June 1843) he had attempted to put the record straight by criticising the selective use made by Ashley of the available evidence, and by demonstrating the excellence of Sunday School and the adequacy of day school provision in the industrial areas of Yorkshire and Lancashire. Baines pointed out that Ashley had highlighted the worst examples drawn from reports which themselves concentrated on identifying problems. These examples, he argued, were not representative of the decent, well-behaved working population and their children. He conceded that Leeds had its proportion of juvenile delinquents, but quoted its mayor to the effect that

> Most of them are the children of idle and profligate parents, who are *attracted to* a large town by the various resources which it offers to enable them to escape regular labour. THEY DO NOT BELONG TO THE WORKING POPULATION OF THE DISTRICT . . . You have my authority for stating that *the young people employed in factories are seldom brought before our local police tribunals*; and the criminal youths so prominently referred to by Lord Ashley, as an important part of our local population, are *not* those who have been educated in our *Sunday Schools* or are trained to labour in our *factories*, but the miserable and neglected children of the most reckless members of society, who have had the most imperfect education, and who have been at an early period initiated into the habits of indolence, profligacy, and vice.

op. cit., Part 6, pp.9–10.

Baines emphasises the important part played by Sunday Schools in the educational provision of the industrial cities. After surveying the statistical evidence he asks:

> Who can calculate the social, moral and religious benefits of establishing a kind of spiritual superintendence on the part of sixty-six thousand teachers, generally taken from the middle class, over four hundred thousand scholars, generally from the working class? What advantage to the teachers themselves, by exercising their virtues! – what advantages to the scholars, in regard to their manners, their feelings, their tastes, their religious knowledge, their regular observance of the Lord's Day, their habit of attending public worship, the enlightening of their consciences, their associations and conduct throughout their future life! Sunday Schools establish a bond of the greatest importance between the two classes of society.
>
> op. cit., Part 6, pp.24–5.

The advantage of being able to educate young people on Sundays in areas where they were needed to work for the rest of the week are obvious. The idea that education can and should be used as means of social control comes through clearly in this passage. Although Baines emphasises the value of the link between social classes that the Sunday Schools provide, his main stress is on the beneficial influence that the middle-class teachers will have on the behaviour and beliefs of their working-class pupils.

A detailed description of the Sunday School system in operation in Manchester is provided by Reach. He visited the Bennett Street Sunday School attached to St Paul's church on the edge of the Ancoats district where many factory workers lived. It is clear from his account that the activities of Sunday Schools were not restricted either to Sundays or to religious education.

The Bennett-street Sunday school is a vast plain
building, fully as large as an ordinary sized cotton
factory, and exhibiting four long ranges of lofty
windows. The number of pupils at present on the
books is 2,611, and the average attendance 2,152. The
number of Sunday scholars who learn writing and
arithmetic, two evenings a week, paying for their
paper, pens and ink, &c., is 260. The number attending
the daily schools and paying twopence per week is
350. The members of the School Funeral Society
amount to 1,804, and of the School Sick Society to
400. The total amount of relief afforded by these
societies since their commencement is upwards of
£7,285. I may add that in one evening in each week
the female scholars are instructed in plain sewing and
housewifery.

Reach, *Manchester and the Textile Districts in 1849*,
p.47.

Sunday Schools were provided by the middle class for the
working class and the same was true in an adult context of
the Mechanics' Institutions, which flourished in the industrial
towns and cities in the first half of the nineteenth century. A
contemporary account of their growth is given by J. W.
Hudson in his *History of Adult Education*, which was
dedicated to Edward Baines. Hudson, the secretary of the
Manchester Athenaeum, identifies the purposes for which the
Mechanics' Institutions were founded. In the case of Leeds,
for example,

THE LEEDS MECHANICS' INSTITUTION was
established at the close of the year 1824, to supply 'to
the mechanics and artizans of Leeds the means of
acquiring a competent knowledge of those branches
of science which are applied to the manufactures of
the town, and for the further purpose of affording
them pleasurable mental relaxation.' . . . In 1831 . . .
twenty lectures on subjects of physical science, and
two on the nature and uses of wool were delivered.

Five thousand nine hundred volumes were issued;
and classes of mathematics, drawing, and chemistry,
attended by one hundred and fifty pupils, were carried
on during the winter months

J. W. Hudson, *The History of Adult Education*
(1851), p.89.

The emphasis is thus mainly utilitarian, to encourage workmen
to acquire a knowledge of science which they could apply in
the workplace. As works of fiction and general literature were
excluded from the library and works of history and biography
opposed by 'some of the influential supporters of the Institution', the notion of 'pleasurable mental relaxation' seems to
have been a rigorous one. Hudson is quite explicit about the
motives behind educational movements on behalf of the
working class. 'By such means,' he says, 'habits of order,
punctuality, and politeness, would be engendered and flow
from thence into all the other relations and departments of
life.' (p.55) At the same time he is forced to concede that
those who attended the Institutions were increasingly not
those for whom they were intended. Acknowledging 'the
universal complaint that Mechanics Institutions are attended
by persons of a higher rank than those for whom they were
designed', he argues that this is because they have been
infiltrated by white-collar workers, themselves escaping from
institutions like the Athenaeums and Literary Institutions
which were dominated by the influence of their employers.
He proposes a solution to this problem in the form of the
provision of a further level of free evening-classes, exclusively
for the lower orders:

> The clerk turns aside from his employer, either from
> respect or humility, and when he joins his companions
> he generally gives utterance to his discontent by an
> intimation that he shall join the Mechanics', for he
> will not subscribe to an institution where 'the governor'
> is present. The same influences are produced in the
> other Institution, the warehouseman, the packer, the
> carter, and the mill-hand shun the society of the clerk

and the foreman, and they in turn quit the Institution which was established expressly for them. The result is made manifest in the classification of the occupation of members of these societies, but wherefore should the educationalist complain, since it only demonstrates the necessity for creating another class of societies, to which the working operative shall alone be admissable. With the increase of population, society has extended and developed itself in new circles, and the requirements of the age, demand for the labouring classes, not only free public libraries, free public news-rooms, free public-lectures, but evening classes, free to the half-educated shopboy, and the unlettered apprentice.

op. cit., 'Preface', p.vii.

This account suggests that the educational segregation of classes was as clear-cut as the residential segregation observed by Engels. The takeover by clerks and foremen of the institutions provided for working men did not necessarily mean though, as Hudson seems to assume, that they were totally excluded from education. As we shall see in the next chapter, working people did not entirely depend upon their betters for their education: there was, in fact, a tradition of working-class self-education and this often embodied an explicitly political dimension.

The accounts of education in the cities provided by Baines and Hudson are optimistic about both its effectiveness and its potential. Although they recognise that provision is not adequate, they describe a wide variety of schools and adult institutions, and they assume that both the quantity and the quality of educational provision is improving. There is, though, evidence that tends to support Lord Ashley's more pessimistic view. Educational provision in the cities in the first half of the nineteenth century was at best piecemeal. Children working in textile factories were the only group for whom some education was compulsory and a number of writers express concern at the number of children growing up in the industrial cities who managed either to avoid education entirely or whose school careers were short and frequently interrupted. The following example comes from a paper given by Mary Carpenter, one of the founders of the Ragged School movement, to the conference of the National Association for the Promotion of Social Science held in Birmingham in 1857.

Whenever educational statistics are taken in any large town an immense discrepancy is discovered between the number of children who are in attendance at school and those who *actually exist.* Some of them are accounted for by being at work, some are at home for domestic purposes. Some are known to the police as pilferers and vagabonds, if nothing worse; and all these it is now happily within the power of our magistrates to consign either to certified reformatories or to industrial schools. But, after these deductions are made, thousands unaccounted for remain . . . It is to these children, who CANNOT or WILL NOT attend the National and British schools, and yet who have not so committed themselves as to be taken to school by the *hand of the law,* that the efforts of the Ragged Schools are directed. And it is these who present a constant hindrance and temptation to evil to honest children attending school, who draw them off and plunge them into crime, themselves often escaping detection by their superior skill and dexterity, who will ever furnish fresh recruits for our reformatories, who even do much indirectly towards lowering the educational status of the labouring classes, as the close proximity of evil ways must do, and *who will form a band of criminals* for the next generation. Words cannot describe the mischief to the State arising from this mass of ignorance, which *must perpetuate itself* unless strongly grappled with. Its *nature* and *amount* cannot be ascertained by any educational statistics, because such children do not present themselves when these are made, but it may be gathered from the fact that, in only one town – that of Liverpool – of 19,336 persons who had been apprehended in nine months ending September 20th, 1856, only 3.00 per cent could

read and write well, and nearly half had no knowledge
of either.

Mary Carpenter, 'On the Relation of Ragged
Schools to the Educational Movement',
*Transactions of the National Association for the
Promotion of Social Science* (1857), pp.227–8.

The link made by Mary Carpenter between inadequate
education and crime is identical to that made by Lord Ashley,
who himself became chairman of the Ragged Schools Union.
The problems of setting up a school in a deprived urban area
for the type of children who so concerned Mary Carpenter
are described by Alfred Alsop, who in addition to his mission
work (see pp.96–7) started a Ragged School in Lombard
Street, Manchester.

> Sunday, April 11th, we had our school in the after-
> noon, eight-four scholars. Again was our patience
> tried to the utmost, and school upset by a little ragged
> urchin getting up the chimney, and before he would
> come out, I was compelled to get him by the heels,
> dragging him forth, grinning at me with his black face,
> saying 'I could na help it.' . . . Tuesday evening,
> April 13th, there were 125 scholars; but of all the filth,
> rags, disorder, and dirt, it would fail description.
> Teaching was out of the question: we made the effort,
> handing out the slates and pencil, but soon found that
> we must call them in, for they tried the quality of the
> slates, and the nature of each others heads, making it
> a complete failure for that night. But we took an extra
> room, thinking that a separation of boys from girls
> would bring about a better state of things. The follow-
> ing week I was ill, having a narrow escape of the brain
> fever, but God in His goodness raised me up, to labour
> again with the handful of helpers.

Alfred Alsop, *Lombard Street and How We Got
There*, n.d., [1870], pp.9–10.

From this account it would seem that educational provision

in the industrial cities was far from complete and still excluded the most deprived in the years immediately before the Education Act of 1870. W. E. Forster, the architect of the 1870 Act, declared his purpose to be 'to bring elementary education within the reach of every English home, aye, and within the reach of those children who have no homes'. (cit. J. S. Maclure (ed.), *Educational Documents, England and Wales, 1816–1968*, 1965, p.104.) Forster's Act was essentially a compromise, but it marks a milestone in both educational and urban history: the board schools that it established became a familiar feature of the urban scene.

4 The Culture of the Cities

The Business Ethos

The industrial cities of the nineteenth century established themselves on the foundation of a new wealth and in doing so they created a new culture. Whereas traditionally the English power structure had reflected the hierarchies of establishment, the manufacturers and business magnates whose energies were released by the Industrial Revolution could claim to have achieved their status through their own initiative. Their economic power was acknowledged as a political reality by the Reform Act of 1832, but the significance of self-achieved wealth as the measure of individual achievement, with the concomitant emphasis on a primarily economic construction of social relationships, involved changes not only in political arrangements but in ways of seeing the world.

In *Past and Present* (1843) Carlyle contrasted modern society, to its considerable disadvantage, with that of the Middle Ages, coining a phrase that Marx was to seize upon. In the Middle Ages, Carlyle argued, relationships between men depended on something other than 'cash-payment': what his contemporaries have to learn is that 'cash-payment is not the sole nexus of man with man'. (*Past and Present*, 1843, Bk III, Ch. 9.) Commentators like Carlyle, Arnold, Ruskin and William Morris were unremitting in their criticism of a society founded upon the accumulation of personal wealth, and consequently of that society's culture, and we have inherited many of their critical attitudes. To many of the Victorians, however, the vast industrial and commercial growth was a sign of achievement, and if their pride in their accomplishments was often expressed in what seem to us uncritical terms it is a consistent feature of contemporary discussion that it was not only the accumulation of wealth that was at issue, but the uses to which it should be put. We cannot understand the dominant culture of the Victorian city unless we recognise not simply that it was a culture based upon private capital, but that it was a culture that affirmed, often vigorously and aggressively, both the rights and the obligations of self-earned wealth.

The most famous expression of the ethic of individual achievement is Samuel Smiles's *Self-Help; with Illustrations of Character and Conduct* (1859). Smiles's book had its origins in a series of lectures which he gave to a young men's mutual improvement society in Leeds, and its chapter titles are in themselves instructive: 'Leaders of Industry – Inventors and Producers', 'Application and Perseverance', 'Energy and Courage', 'Men of Business', 'Money – Its Use and Abuse'. Another populist exponent of these values was James Burnley, a Yorkshire author, who in *The Romance of Modern Industry* (1889) surveyed the achievements of industry since the Industrial Revolution. Burnley wrote a number of works, including a novel, *Looking for the Dawn* (1874), based on his knowledge of Bradford. Writing towards the end of the century, he allows his 'retrospective glance' to take in a range of examples of commercial and industrial achievement, and these he always evaluates in economic terms. Thus his chapter on 'Gigantic Businesses' records the expansion of the Lancashire cotton trade, of the West Riding woollen trade, and of Birmingham and Sheffield, 'paramount in the hardware community': in doing so he gives precise details of the enormous fortunes achieved by the leaders of the various industries. Later he chronicles the individual careers of 'Some Modern Millionaires': and his account of the career of the Manchester cotton merchant John Rylands is a spectacular example of the kind of achievement possible in the industrial communities in the nineteenth century:

> Among the many millionaires whose coffers have been filled to overflowing by the growth of the cotton trade of Lancashire, one of the most notable is Mr John Rylands, by whose energy and wonderful business tact the present firm of Rylands & Sons, Limited, was pioneered to the highest prosperity. Mr Rylands, who has just died in the ninetieth year of his age, had a career of surprising activity. From a boy he displayed

a striking aptitude for commercial pursuits, and at the age of seventeen was partner with his father and brother at Wigan. While they attended to the manufacturing concern at home, he travelled through North Wales, Cheshire and Shropshire, as well as Lancashire and Yorkshire, seeking orders, carrying his patterns about in his saddle-bags. In 1822 he started a warehouse in Manchester, and a large business was rapidly developed there. Two years later the firm erected a spinning mill and dyeing and bleaching works near Wigan, and from modest beginnings the concern was expanded until it became of vast proportions. Other mills were started in subsequent years, the largest being situated at Gorton. The latter was purchased in 1864, and covered 16,000 square yards of land. The spinning shed contained 32,000 throstles and 31,000 mule spindles, producing 75,000 lbs of yarn every week. The weaving shed contained 1500 power looms. The firm's turnover to-day is reckoned by millions per annum. As general merchants, spinners, manufacturers, bleachers, dyers, and colliery-owners, the firm employs upwards of 11,000 persons. Their spinning and weaving mills now number seventeen establishments, representing an aggregate of 200,000 spindles and 5000 looms. At Bolton the firm make dimities, damasks, toilet cloths, and quilts; at Chorley, floor oil-cloths; at Crawshawbooth, grey calicoes; at Gorton, Dacca calicoes, twills, jeanettes, and shirtings; at Heapley they scour, bleach, and dye the Dacca calicoes and silesias; in Wormwood Street, London, they manufacture clothing; in Commercial Road, London, shirts; at Swinton Bowers, regattas, Oxfords, and ticks; at Wigan, Dacca calicoes; while at the Longford and Medlock Works, and at the Water Street Mills, all in Manchester, and at the clothing manufactory at Crewe, they employ an immense number of people in making underclothing, corsets, umbrellas, collars, and so forth. Then the Manchester warehouse of the firm forms one of the most magnificent commercial buildings in the world. It consists of eight stories, and covers an area of seven acres. Mr John Rylands was the chief organising mind in working up this enormous business, and it would be strange indeed if he were not to be reckoned amongst the chief commercial millionaires of this country. He was all along a man of action and determination, not wanting in politeness or courtesy, but having an abhorence of unnecessary talk. It is said of him that once upon a time he silenced a long-winded traveller by bluntly observing, 'My good man, if you can afford to waste your words, I can't afford to waste my time; it is very precious – worth, in fact, nearly a guinea a minute. Good Day!'

> James Burnley, *The Romance of Modern Industry*
> (1889) pp.270–71.

The success which accumulated for Rylands in the second half of the century was clearly a reward for that 'striking aptitude for commercial pursuits' that marked his youth: the character sketch which concludes Burnley's account, with its telling anecdote about the value of a busy man's time, confirms the impression of a man whose life from his earlist days was devoted exclusively to business.

The industrial cities were first and foremost business communities, their leading citizens great magnates of industry and commerce. Cooke Taylor, in his account of the Manchester of the early 1840s, describes the city as 'essentially a place of business, where pleasure is unknown as a pursuit, and amusements scarcely rank as secondary considerations'. Of its inhabitants he says that 'the men are as businesslike as the place', and he identifies the Cotton Exchange as the place where the character of Manchester can be best understood:

Were I asked how a stranger could best form a notion of the character of the Manchester manufacturers, I should recommend him to visit the Exchange of Manchester at the period of 'high change'; that is, about noon on a Tuesday. It is the parliament of the lords of cotton – their legislative assembly – which enacts laws as immutable as those of the Medes and

Persians, but, unlike every other parliament in the
world, very much is done and very little is said . . .
Transactions of immense extent are conducted by
nods, winks, shrugs, or brief phrases, compared to
which the laconisms of the ancient Spartans were
specimens of tediousness and verbosity . . . The
characteristic feature of the assembly is talent and
intelligence in high working order; genius and stupidity
appear to be equally absent; but if the average of
intellect be not very high, it is evident that not a
particle of it remains unemployed.

> W. Cooke Taylor, *Notes of a Tour in the
> Manufacturing Districts of Lancashire* (1842,
> reprinted with Introduction by W. H. Chaloner,
> 1968), pp.9, 10–11.

Cooke Taylor's emphasis on the earnestness of the Manchester
businessmen – and on their taciturnity – confirms Burnley's
account of John Rylands. Mrs Gaskell, in her fictional account
in *North and South*, couples the earnestness with a new kind
of confidence. Her heroine, Margaret Hale, finds herself at
dinner with a group of businessmen who explain their methods
to a stranger:

Mr Horsfall, the stranger, whose visit to the town was
the original germ of the party, was asking questions
relative to the trade and manufactures of the place;
and the rest of the gentlemen – all Milton men – were
giving him answers and explanations. Some dispute
arose, which was warmly contested; it was referred to
Mr Thornton, who had hardly spoken before; but
who now gave an opinion, the grounds of which were
so clearly stated that even the opponents yielded.
Margaret's attention was thus called to her host; his
whole manner, as master of the house, and entertainer
of his friends, was so straightforward, yet simple and
modest, as to be thoroughly dignified.

> *North and South*, Ch. 20.

Margaret, new to the city from the south of England, 'was surprised to think how much she enjoyed this dinner.' She,

> liked the exultation in the sense of power which these Milton men had. It might be rather rampant in its display, and savour of boasting; but still they seemed to defy the old limits of possibility, in a kind of fine intoxication, caused by the recollection of what had been achieved, and what yet should be.
>
> Ibid.

Boastful or silent, though, the devotion to business is absolute, and 'southern' civilities have to yield pride of place to northern energy and commitment.

Civic Pride

A further account of the Manchester business ethos appears in the opening chapter of a guide book to Manchester published in 1839, B. Love's *Manchester As It Is*. Written as an answer to all those accounts of Manchester then circulating which drew attention to its problematic nature, Love's book emphasises the positive aspects of the city, which he sees as being firmly founded on the achievements of its businessmen, whose behaviour he defines in terms identical to those of Cooke Taylor:

> The habits of Manchester men of business are marked by the utmost perseverance and energy. Unlike the merchants of London or of Scotland (as we are informed), they permit little relaxation to be associated with the stern demands of business. With the exception of a week's or a fortnight's holiday at Southport or a trip to Wales, during the year, nothing but sickness is allowed to interfere with a daily attendance to the business of commerce or manufactures. And this attention is not for a few hours only in the day; it

commences early in the morning, and is protracted to
a late hour in the evening. It is a common thing to see
the leading merchants of the town – some of them
possessed of wealth to the amount of a quarter of a
million sterling – posting from their country villas to
their counting houses between eight and nine o'clock
in the morning; and many of them do not return home
(except to a hasty dinner) till nine or ten o'clock in
the evening. Business becomes a habit; and this habit
becomes a pleasure; and on this account – more than
from mere love of gain – they are impelled to proceed
onwards in a vocation which, on account of its
enterprise and excitement, presents to them the greatest
of earthly charms.

B. Love, *Manchester As It Is* (1839), pp.37–8.

Love's book is primarily a work of advertisement for a city
whose reputation was threatening to become one solely of
social squalor and human suffering. His emphasis therefore
is on the city's achievements, not simply in terms of its
commercial success but of its cultural institutions, its architecture, and its philanthropic provision for all classes of society.
All these he sees as being directly related to its thriving
economy:

Besides increasing rapidly in extent, the towns of
Manchester and Salford are annually improving in the
elegance of their appearance . . . Many important
alterations have already taken place, and many others
are in contemplation. The spirit of improvement is
contagious, and from the 'Improvement Committee'
of the police commissioners it has spread among private
individuals. Owners of property come forward to meet
the proposals of the 'Committee of Improvement';
and, consequently, widened streets become ornamented with good houses. Market-street is a notable
example: from a dirty narrow lane, it has been conver-
ted into one of the handsomest streets in England.

op. cit. pp.19–20.

It is typical of Love that he should use the city's main commercial street to exemplify his argument; throughout his guide he insists on the social benefits of private wealth. 'That this attention to business is consistent with – what is by some persons considered incompatible – the utmost liberality, the many noble charitable institutions the town can boast of, is sufficient evidence', he says (p.38), and he takes care to describe these institutions in detail. Later, Manchester was to be famous for its great neo-Gothic Town Hall, commissioned in 1867 and finally completed in 1880, but at this stage in the city's development its most striking examples of architectural grandeur were for the most part to be found in its commercial buildings – its mills, its warehouses and its exchanges, all of which Love records and enthusiastically describes.

Manchester As It Is is a typical production of its period. One of the indications of the cities' growing consciousness of their own identities is the number of historical and topographical works about them produced within their own communities. Civic pride developed at a different pace in different places. Buildings appropriate to their new sense of status were appearing in all the major cities from the first decades of the century, but when the immigrant woollen manufacturer Jacob Behrens moved from Leeds to Bradford in 1838 he found the latter an impoverished city compared with the one he had left. (cf. *Memoirs of Sir Jacob Behrens*, 1885.) Some years later, however, Bradford's commissioning of a new exchange building was to call from Ruskin, to whom the city's businessmen had turned for advice, one of his most memorable attacks on civic architecture as an expression of the commercial spirit:

> In a word then, I do not care about this Exchange – because *you* don't; and because you know perfectly well I cannot make you. Look at the essential con- ditions of the case, which you, as business men, know perfectly well, though perhaps you think I forget them. You are going to spend £30,000, which to you, collectively, is nothing; the buying of a new coat, is, to the cost of it, a much more important matter of consideration, to me, than building a new Exchange

is to you. But you think you may as well have the
right thing for your money. You know there are a
great many odd styles of architecture about; you don't
want to do anything ridiculous; you hear of me, among
others, as a respectable architectural milliner; and you
send for me, that I may tell you the leading fashion;
and what is, in our shops, for the moment, the newest
and sweetest thing in pinnacles.

John Ruskin, *The Crown of Wild Olive* (1866),
Lecture ii, para.53.

Ruskin, for whom 'all good architecture is the expression of
national life and character', and who often took a very dubious
view of the life and character of his contemporaries, constantly
inveighed against the use of architectural ornamentation on
buildings which he believed could only express the worst
aspects of *laissez-faire* capitalism. The Bradford businessmen
had to listen to him in the heart of their own city, but when
he had gone they built their Exchange and three years later,
followed it up with a competition for a new town hall.

The civic pride which reflected itself in the commercial
buildings of the cities transferred itself to their public buildings. Philanthropy built hospitals, bath houses, libraries,
public lecture halls and sometimes theatres; the expansion of
civic administration led to the building of new town halls –
even, sometimes, where such buildings had only recently
been built. Manchester's first nineteenth-century town hall,
for example, was built in 1822–5, and superseded by Water-
house's famous neo-Gothic building begun in 1868; Birmingham's first town hall of 1834–49 was never adequate to
its administrative function and a new Council House was
begun in 1874. Such developments reflect both the realities
of urban expansion and the symbolism of civic pride: amongst
the major – and many of the minor – towns and cities there
was certainly a strongly competitive element in the impulse
to erect buildings worthy of the communities they served. In
Chapter 2 we cited Dickens's Mr Pecksniff as an example of
the boost given to the architectural profession by urban
expansion: in *Martin Chuzzlewit* Pecksniff's greatest triumph

comes when the foundation stone is laid for a new public building which he fraudulently claims to have designed. Dickens's description of the event satirises the pretensions both of the architect and of the civic dignitaries who have given him his commission and who share in his triumph:

> The charity school, in clean linen, came filing in two and two, so much to the self-approval of all the people present who didn't subscribe to it, that many of them shed tears. A band of music followed, led by a conscientious drummer who never left off. Then came a great many gentlemen with wands in their hands, and bows on their breasts, whose share in the proceedings did not appear to be distinctly laid down, and who trod upon each other, and blocked up the entry for a considerable period. These were followed by the Mayor and Corporation, all clustering round the member for the Gentlemanly Interest; who had the great Mr Pecksniff, the celebrated architect, on his right hand, and conversed with him familiarly as they came along. Then the ladies waved their handkerchiefs, and the gentlemen their hats, and the charity children shrieked, and the member for the Gentlemanly Interest bowed . . . Now a silver trowel was brought; and when the member for the Gentlemanly Interest, tucking up his coat-sleeve, did a little sleight of hand with the mortar, the air was rent, so loud was the applause. The workman-like manner in which he did it was amazing. No one could conceive where such a gentlemanly creature could have picked the knowledge up.
>
> When he had made a kind of dirt-pie under the direction of the mason, they brought up a little vase containing coins, the which the member for the Gentlemanly Interest jingled, as if he were going to conjure. Whereat they said how droll, how cheerful, what a flow of spirits! This put into its place, an ancient scholar read the inscription, which was in Latin: not in English: that would never do. It gave great satisfaction; especially every time there was a good long substantive in the third declension, ablative

case, with an adjective to match; at which periods the
assembly became very tender, and were much affected.

Martin Chuzzlewit, Ch. 35.

Dickens does not specify either the town where this ceremony
takes place, or the function of the building. It is clear from
the events of the novel though that it is Liverpool, and it may
not be entirely a coincidence that Dickens himself, like the
novel's eponymous hero, passed through Liverpool on his
way to and from the United States in the early 1840s. It was
at precisely this time that Liverpool's St George's Hall, a
building which set the standard for much of the town hall
building that was to follow, was being built. In *Victorian
Cities* Asa Briggs takes the building of Leeds Town Hall as
his example of this kind of expression of civic pride, and gives
a detailed account of the various conflicts of interest that were
involved. In particular, Briggs emphasises the way in which
the need for a symbolic expression of the city's identity
triumphed, albeit with difficulty, over the objections of
the more cost-conscious factions amongst the city's leading
figures. He records that in 1854 J. D. Heaton, a distinguished
physician and city dignitary, was called on to give a paper at
the Leeds Literary and Philosophical Society to justify the
project, then already well under way. Heaton's remarks show
very clearly the kind of feeling that found expression in such
a grandiose building as the proposed town hall, and throw a
positive light upon those aspirations towards municipal dignity which Dickens ridiculed:

> The municipal buildings about to be erected by the
> burgesses of Leeds, besides the primary object of
> furnishing convenient accommodation to their officers
> in the transaction of public business, are intended to
> present an appearance worthy of the wealth and
> prosperity of the town; to show that in the ardour of
> mercantile pursuits the inhabitants of Leeds have not
> omitted to cultivate the perception of the beautiful and
> a taste for the fine arts, and to serve as a lasting

monument of their public spirit and generous pride in the possession of their municipal privileges. They will form a monument which shall present an object of beauty not merely for their own contemplation and that of their children for successive generations, but which may be famous beyond their own limits, and, like the noble halls of France, of Belgium and of Italy, may attract to our town the visits of strangers, dilettanti tourists, and the lovers of art from distant places.

We have seen how the citizens of free towns in the middle ages erected for their public meetings, and as the seat and outward symbol of their public government, the most sumptuous buildings, decorated with all the grace which architecture and sculpture could confer upon the exterior, and whose interior halls added to these effects the rich variety of colour which the painter's art supplies. With the selection of the architectural designs for our Town Hall now in course of erection, I believe the inhabitants of Leeds have expressed a very general sentiment of approval and satisfaction. And perhaps it is not too much to anticipate that the completion of its construction will not be the end of the work, but that in it the memory of our Leeds worthies, and of the great men of our country, may be hereafter preserved by the statuary's art, and that native artists may depict upon its inner walls the more memorable events in the history of our town and country, the progress of manufactures and of our commercial prosperity. The work has been begun in no merely utilitarian or unduly economic spirit, and I trust that the same enlightened liberality and taste will watch over its progress, and still from year to year, and indeed from century to century, add to its embellishment and completeness.

J. Wemyss Reid, *A Memoir of John Deakin Heaton, M.D., of Leeds* (1883), pp.147–9.

Heaton's appeal to the example of the Middle Ages is an interesting gloss on the tendency of writers like Carlyle and

Ruskin to make similar cultural comparisons at the expense
of their contemporaries. Cuthbert Brodrick, the architect for
the building, had visited the kind of medieval cities to which
Heaton refers, and his design, in reflecting this experience,
set a pattern for some of the more flamboyant town halls –
most notably, of course, that of Manchester – that were to
follow. It was Manchester too, rather than Leeds, which
was to follow Heaton's suggestions for decorative murals
exemplifying great moments of local and national history.
But Leeds Town Hall was a building which in every way
justified the aspirations of those who planned it. When the
Queen came to its official opening, the order of service
included a prayer that Almighty God would 'grant that
the completion of this hall may contribute to the glory of
Thy Name and to the lasting welfare of the inhabitants of
this town'. The inhabitants of the town, at least, were not
disappointed. The local newspaper, the *Leeds Intelligencer*,
was able to quote *The Times* to the effect that 'after every
objection is made, the plain fact remains that the new Leeds
Town Hall has, of its kind no superior in England, and very
few in Europe.' (*Leeds Intelligencer*, 11 September 1858.)

Victorian town halls were not simply, or even primarily,
centres of administration. They were conceived as often as
not as centres, practical as well as symbolic, of every kind of
civic activity. Thus, in its own appraisal of the Leeds building,
the *Leeds Intelligencer* commended it for the way it would
fulfil a multi-functional purpose:

> For municipal purposes it has been spoken of as
> unrivalled; and for the administration of justice, for
> large assemblies of the people on questions of exciting
> interest, for literary and scientific gatherings, for
> soirées, for musical entertainments, and for every
> object which can tend to elevate and civilize the
> manners of the people, it affords facilities which are
> not exceeded in any town in the country, and are very
> rarely combined in any edifice.
>
> Ibid.

Civic functions were as much an expression of civic pride as the buildings themselves: no town hall would have been complete without its organ. Concerts, indeed, were a particularly popular expression of municipal enthusiasm: it was through Birmingham's association with Mendelssohn, for example, that the first performance of his oratorio *Elijah* was given in the town hall with the composer himself conducting in 1846. Local Corporations devised public ceremonies at every opportunity. As we have seen, Dickens was an early critic of municipal pretension, but he was not slow to respond to invitations to speak on such occasions, invariably using them to express his sympathy for practical democracy, particularly when it took on an educational dimension. Given the passage from *Martin Chuzzlewit* which we cited earlier, there is a nice irony in finding him at the end of his life proposing the toast to the mayor and corporation in Liverpool's St George's Hall:

> I have now, ladies and gentlemen, to propose to you a toast inseparable from the enterprise of Liverpool – from the public honour and spirit of Liverpool; equally inseparable from the stately streets and buildings around us, and from the hospitals, schools and free libraries, and those great monuments of consideration for the many which have made this place an example to England. I have to propose to you to drink 'His Worship the Mayor and the Corporation of this town.'
>
> K. J. Fielding, ed., *The Speeches of Charles Dickens* (1960), p.392.

What Dickens, in fictional mode, might have made of such a speech it is not difficult to imagine. But, in context, his rhetoric is not inappropriate. Over the period of Dickens's adult career the kind of buildings he refers to had proliferated: they still stand as monuments to Victorian civic pride.

Middle-class Culture

In *Culture and Anarchy* (1869) Matthew Arnold addressed himself to the question of the culture of his contemporaries, and in doing so produced his famous re-definition of the English class structure. For the aristocracy Arnold coined the term 'Barbarians', the middle classes, he referred to as 'Philistines' and the working class as the 'Populace'. These he conceived as deliberately ironic terms, particularly in the case of his 'Philistines' who, by his analysis, were emerging as the dominant class. For Arnold the English business and commercial classes were a new force: their culture – or in his terms lack of it – he conceived of as a threat to civilised values. Preoccupied with the business of making money, rigidly adhering to the economic doctrines of *laissez-faire* and the religious practices of Dissent, they had neither time nor sympathy for what Arnold defined as culture: 'a pursuit of our total perfection by means of getting to know, on all the matters which most concern us, the best which has been thought and said in the world'. (*Culture and Anarchy*, 1869, 'Preface'.) Arnold was scornful of the habits of mind and behaviour of these 'Philistines': they had no culture of their own, and to consider them in the light of culture was to recognise the nature of the threat they posed.

Arnold's analysis is open to criticism on various counts. In particular, his own definition of culture is obviously partial and class based: as such it is likely to be hostile to alternative cultural experience. Nevertheless, when we turn to specific accounts of the life-style of the manufacturing and business class, it is not difficult to find support for his claim that, by traditional standards, it could be regarded as culturally impoverished and, indeed, in the early stages of the commercial boom and unrestrained by religious or moral inhibitions, more so than he suggests. Peter Gaskell, a Manchester commentator of the 1830s, writes of the habits of mill-owners who have only recently risen from a labouring background:

> Master cotton-spinners and weavers, at the commencement of this important epoch, were in many instances men sprung from the ranks of the labourers, or from

a grade just removed above these – uneducated – of coarse habits – sensual in their enjoyments – partaking of the rude revelry of their dependants – overwhelmed by success – but yet, paradoxical as it may sound, industrious men, and active and far-sighted tradesmen. Many of these might be found, after a night spent in debauchery and licentiousness, sobered down by an hour or two of rest, and by the ringing of the factory bell, going through the business of the day with untiring activity and unerring rectitude – surrounded too, as they were, by their companions, alike busily engaged under their inspection – again to plunge, at the expiration of the hours of labour, in the same vortex of inebriation and riot.

> P. Gaskell. *The Manufacturing Population of England* (1833, reprinted 1974), p.55.

Clearly we should not exaggerate the quality of cultural life amongst the middle class in the industrial cities, certainly in the earlier part of the period. The novelists, however, tell a rather different story. Dickens's Thomas Gradgrind, in *Hard Times*, is certainly resistant to literature and the arts, but on strictly ideological grounds and not because of self-indulgence. He is 'A man of realities. A man of facts and calculations. A man who proceeds on the principle that two and two are four, and nothing over, and who is not to be talked into allowing for anything over.' (*Hard Times*, Ch. 2.) To this extent he tends to confirm the Arnoldian stereotype. A rather different, if romanticised, insight into the cultural attainments of an industrial magnate is offered by Disraeli in *Coningsby* (1844). As part of his formative experience, Disraeli takes his hero, an Etonian aristocrat, to Manchester, from where he travels to inspect the factories of the cotton manufacturer Millbank, set in a model village 'about three miles from Bolton'. When they meet, Coningsby is surprised not only by the scale and elegance of Millbank's house – 'a capacious and classic hall; at the end a staircase in the Italian fashion' – but by the civility of his host who in justification of his belief in progress engages him in an extended and informed discussion of the English historical tradition. Millbank's dining-room is an appropriate setting for the discussion:

> The walls of the dining-room were covered with pictures of great merit, all of the modern English school. Mr. Millbank understood no other, he was wont to say, and he found that many of his friends who did, bought a great many pleasing pictures that were copies, and many originals that were very displeasing. He loved a fine free landscape by Lee, that gave him the broad plains, the green lanes, and running streams of his own land; a group of animals by Landseer, as full of speech and sentiment as if they were designed by Aesop; above all, he delighted in the household humour and homely pathos of Wilkie. And if a higher tone of imagination pleased him, he could gratify it without difficulty among his favourite masters. He possessed some specimens of Etty worthy of Venice when it was alive; he could muse amid the twilight ruins of ancient cities raised by the magic pencil of Danby, or accompany a group of fair Neapolitans to a festival by the genial aid of Unwins.
>
> Benjamin Disraeli, *Coningsby* (1844), Bk IV,
> Ch. 4.

If some of these artistic preferences have failed to stand the test of time, that hardly undermines the point being made. The manufacturer is presented as a man of substantial culture, whose tastes reflect the independence of his views.

During his stay with the industrialist Coningsby finds himself in conversation with his daughter who is stitching pin-cushions 'for a fancy fair about to be held in aid of that excellent institution, the Manchester Athenaeum' (ibid.). The existence of such institutions in the major provincial cities testifies to the way in which they evolved their own distinctive traditions of intellectual life. The anonymous author of *The Stranger in Liverpool*, an early civic guide-book like Love's *Manchester As It Is*, emphasises the way in which his city has set precedents followed elsewhere. First it specifies the Liverpool Athenaeum:

> This institution, the first of the kind established in this kingdom, and which has given birth to similar ones in London, Bath, Bristol &c. is situate in Church Street. It is a neat stone building, consisting of a library and a newsroom.
>
> It contains upwards of 10,000 volumes, the whole of which have been collected in the short space of twenty-three years. The books are not permitted to be taken out of the library, but the subscribers have access to them the whole of the day, and the room is filled up with proper accommodation for the readers; the subscribers have also the privilege of introducing a friend, provided he is not a resident in the town. Adjoining the library is a committee-room, and apartments for the accommodation of the librarian. The appearance of the room is respectable and pleasing. and, from the works being more carefully used than if permitted to circulate, this institution bids fair to stand a lasting monument to the taste and liberality of the inhabitants of Liverpool.
>
> *The Stranger in Liverpool* (1823), pp.99–100

Liverpool's Athenaeum was founded in 1799; to it the author of *The Stranger in Liverpool* was able to add the Lyceum 'furnished with a large collection of London, provincial and Irish newspapers; with numerous magazines, reviews, maps, &c.', the Union newsroom, the Exchange newsroom with its 'Ionic columns, the shaft of which is composed of one entire and beautiful stone; a singularity not easy to be paralleled in this species of architecture', and the Liverpool Royal Institution, founded in 1814. The account of this last explicitly relates its foundation to the perceived educational and cultural needs of a growing urban community:

> Its object is the promotion of literature, science and the arts . . . The following extract from a statement

published by the committee, in 1814, will still further elucidate the object and plan of the institution:

'Liverpool having tripled its population within the last forty years, and now containing, with the adjacent villages, at least 110,000 inhabitants, additional means of instruction are required for completing the education of youth, which may not only relieve parents from the expense and anxiety of sending their children to a distance, but might induce strangers to bring their families here for that purpose from different parts of the district with which it is connected; especially such as may intend their sons for trade, as they could then unite here, in some measure, scientific with commercial education.'

op. cit., pp.105–6.

The Royal Institution was not only to be a school however:

'In order to induce men of science to fix their residence, and become teachers in Liverpool, it is proposed to establish a fund, from which such remuneration as may be necessary might be afforded to them for delivering lectures and instruction in different branches of literature and science. These lectures are intended not only for the instruction of youth, but also as a rational source of information and recreation for persons further advanced in life, who may thus be made acquainted, in the most satisfactory and interesting manner, with the rapid progress of literature and science which characterises the present age.'

Ibid.

In their development of institutions such as these – libraries, newsrooms, educational and learned societies and associations – the cities were often building upon already existing foundations. The Liverpool Royal Institution, for example, housed the city's Literary and Philosophical Society, and although in Liverpool's case this was of recent foundation, the famous Literary and Philosophical Societies – those of

Newcastle, for example, and of Manchester, which provided a forum for the career of the chemist John Dalton in exactly the way prescribed in the above account – had been founded in the previous century as expressions of the spirit of the Enlightenment. It was not until later in the century that the new civic universities could provide chairs and departments for men such as Dalton, but the development of the industrial towns and cities, with their newly aware middle class, rapidly accelerated the process that such societies had initiated; furthermore the functional link between science and industry confirmed a new set of cultural priorities. In the course of time the process was extended to include the daughters, as well as the sons of the middle classes. The North of England Council for Promoting the Higher Education of Women, which was established in 1867, arranged for university lecturers to deliver courses of lectures in the industrial cities. James Stuart, of Trinity College, Cambridge, recalls:

In the autumn of 1867 I lectured on Physical Astronomy to four classes of ladies in Liverpool, Leeds, Manchester and Sheffield, numbering respectively, 80, 100, 160 and 200 . . . The questions which were asked of me were in general very much to the point . . . Of the papers which I received some were pre-eminently good, and the average of the papers showed a thorough appreciation of the subject.

J. Stuart, 'The Teaching of Science', J. E. Butler, (ed.), *Woman's Work and Woman's Culture* (1869), pp.128–9.

Given the expansion of this kind of activity it is clear that not only was there an active intellectual middle class in the towns and cities of industrial England in the early years of the nineteenth century, but that it was establishing its own priorities and standards.

Working-class Culture

One of the most famous poems of working-class experience of the nineteenth century, J. C. Prince's 'The Death of the Factory Child', describes the scene in a factory town at the end of the working day:

> While yet the night was boisterous and chill –
> While winds were loud, and snows were drifting still,
> The bell gave out its long expected sound,
> The mighty engine ceased its weary round.
> Forth rushed the captives, – a degraded train! –
> Till morn should summon them to toil again.
> Some to the maddening ale-cup rashly sped;
> Some to the short oblivion of their bed.

> J. C. Prince, 'The Death of the Factory Child',
> *Hours with the Muses* (1841).

Prince was only one of a number of artisan poets whose work, as he said of his own poems, created an 'extraordinary interest . . . (not) attributable to the merits of the Poems themselves', but to the way in which they advocated 'the rights' and elevated 'the tastes and pursuits of his labouring fellow-countrymen'. (J. C. Prince, *Hours with the Muses*, 'Preface', 2nd. edn, 1841, cit. B. Maidment, ed., *The Poorhouse Fugitives*, 1987, p.339.) The work of these poets was in itself an expression of a distinctive working-class culture, but what their poems reflect, above all, is lives subjected to the unrelenting pressure of the demands of work and basic subsistence, and with apparently little opportunity to indulge 'tastes and pursuits' of any but the most rudimentary kind. Prince's account of the workers speeding to the 'maddening ale-cup' after the exhaustion of their daily toil, for example, is enlarged upon by another of the artisan poets, Thomas Cleaver:

> Now where the tavern swells its motley din,
> Dispute and song discordant reign within;
> The Brain is tortured for the ribald jest;

If wit be dull, the laugh supplies the rest;
There seeks the troubled mind a fair repose,
Woos in the cup oblivion of its woes.
The politician prompts the keen debate,
Reforms the laws and renovates the State.
See, there the man debased – the spendthrift sot,
While by his hearth, forsaken and forgot,
Pines the lone form of her, the grief-distressed,
Her cherub infant sleeping at her breast
Turns her said eye to days when all was bright,
And weeps and watches through the weary night.

Thomas Cleaver, 'Night', from *'Night' and Other
Poems* (1848).

The dismissive reference to political activism – public houses
were often a venue for the political culture of the working
class – together with the sentimentality focussed upon the
suffering wife, shows that Cleaver, like many of the working-
class poets, came to endorse deeply conservative values, but
his basic point cannot be rejected: the life of the working
man would seem to have left little space for self-cultivation
of any kind. What is remarkable is that the history of the
industrial working class in the first half of the nineteenth
century, both as recorded by middle-class observers, and as
documented in the publications of working-class writers
themselves, tells a very different story. Many of the working-
class poets would seem to have tempered their sense of
injustice with a quietism expressed both directly and in the
traditional forms they adopted, but consideration of a wider
range of working-class publications – pamphlets, newspapers
and autobiographies, for example – reveals a very different
political spirit. From his Manchester viewpoint Engels drew
attention to the strength of working-class intellectualism, and
argued that, drawing on radically different sources, it was
directly opposed to the culture of the bourgeoisie:

> No better evidence of the extent to which the English
> workers have succeeded in educating themselves can
> be brought forward than the fact that the most import-
> ant modern works in philosophy, poetry and politics

are in practice read only by the proletariat. The
middle classes, enslaved by the influences generated
by their environment, are blinded by prejudice. They
are horror-stricken at the very idea of reading anything of a really progressive nature. The working
classes, on the other hand, have no such stupid inhibitions and devour such works with pleasure and profit.

The Condition of the Working Classes in England,
p.272

Engels, here as elsewhere, over-simplifies, but his polarisation
of the distinction between two kinds of culture is a reminder
that not only should we not judge working-class culture by
the degree of its conformity to middle-class standards, but
that it presents us with its own powerful alternative traditions.
The conflict between conformity and radicalism is central to
any consideration of working-class culture and it reflects itself
in a number of ways – in the attitudes towards working-class
intellectualism expressed by middle-class writers, for example;
in the debates over the kind of provision in the towns and cities
that should be made for working-class self-improvement; and
in the far from consistent positions adopted by working-class
leaders themselves.

The most explicit testimony in fiction to the pervasiveness
of working-class cultural activity appears in *Mary Barton*, in
a chapter where Mrs Gaskell introduces an old spinner, Job
Legh, who has devoted all of his spare time to entomology.
Job Legh, she tells us, is representative of a class:

There is a class of men in Manchester, unknown even
to many of the inhabitants, and whose existence will
probably be doubted by many, who yet may claim
kindred with all the noble names that science recogni-
zes. I said 'in Manchester', but they are scattered all
over the manufacturing districts of Lancashire. In the
neighbourhood of Oldham there are weavers, common
handloom weavers, who throw the shuttle with unceas-
ing sound, though Newton's 'Principia' lie open on
the loom, to be snatched at in work hours, but revelled

over in meal times, or at night. Mathematical problems are received with interest, and studied with absorbing attention by many a broad-spoken, common-looking factory-hand. It is perhaps less astonishing that the most popularly interesting branches of natural history have their warm and devoted followers among this class. There are botanists among them, equally familiar with either the Linnaean or the Natural system, who know the name and habitat of every plant within a day's walk from their dwellings; who steal the holiday of a day or two when any particular plant should be in flower, and tying up their simple food in their pocket-handkerchiefs, set off with single purpose to fetch home the humble-looking weed. There are entomologists, who may be seen with a rude-looking net, ready to catch any winged insect, or a kind of dredge, with which they rake the green and slimy pools; practical, shrewd, hard-working men, who pore over every new specimen with real scientific delight.

Mary Barton, Ch. 5.

Mrs Gaskell goes on to document her account with examples of specific contributions to scientific scholarship made by these amateur enthusiasts, the 'thoughtful, little understood, working men of Manchester', and she provides an appropriate cultural foil for Job Legh in the figure of his grand-daughter Margaret, a blind singer of rare talent, familiar with both local folk-song and sacred oratorio. Both characters testify movingly to the capacity of the working-class, in spite of their deprivation, to achieve cultural enrichment. In citing Job Legh as her example of working-class culture, however, Mrs Gaskell deliberately chooses an example of a working man whose intellectualism can be seen as a diversion from the life and problems of the work-place. In this he stands in direct opposition to her original hero in the novel, John Barton, whose self-educated political activism leads him ultimately to murder.

The extent to which Mrs Gaskell, in her example of Job Legh, has separated the intellectual life from the circumstances of the work-place, is apparent when we consider how the history of the Industrial Revolution is, for a large part, the history of self-educated men. The founding fathers of industrialism – Arkwright, Brindley, Watt, later George Stephenson – were men who had harnessed their intellectual energies to the practicalities of work and production; in that sense industrialism itself provided opportunities for self-educated men that might otherwise have been unavailable. Samuel Smiles's *Lives of the Engineers* (1861–2) was to offer the great engineers as role-models to a later generation: a similar spirit is expressed in these lines by Ebenezer Elliott, the author of *Corn-Law Rhymes* (1831):

> No; there he moves, the thoughtful engineer,
> The soul of all this motion; rule in hand,
> And coarsely apron'd – simple, plain, sincere –
> An honest man; self-taught to understand
> The useful wonders which he built and plann'd.
> Self-taught to read and write – a poor man's son,
> Though poor no more – how would he sit alone
> When the hard labour of the day was done,
> Bent o'er his table, silent as a stone,
> To make the wisdom of the wise his own!
> How oft of Brindley's deeds th'apprenticed boy
> Would speak delighted, long ere freedom came!
> And talk of Watt! while, shedding tears of joy,
> His widow'd mother heard, and hoped the name
> Of her poor boy, like theirs, would rise to fame.

> Ebenezer Elliott, 'Steam at Sheffield', *Poetical Works* (1840–1).

Elliott was a self-taught poet who had himself set up in business in the iron industry in Sheffield: Carlyle, in a review, reflected on the remarkable fact that 'a Sheffield worker in brass and iron . . . whose first grand problem and obligation was nowise spiritual culture, but hard labour for his daily bread' should achieve more of 'real culture' than his socially advantaged superiors. (Thomas Carlyle, 'Corn-Law Rhymes', *Edinburgh Review*, July 1832.)

Elliott's lines are based upon direct experience: they show how working-class enthusiasm could be integrated with work itself. His engineer is not, like Mrs Gaskell's enthusiasts, snatching the opportunity for self-improvement in brief moments of holiday, but relating his self-education to the demands of the work-place. Similar experience is recorded by a working-class autobiographer, George Jacob Holyoake, in his account of his early life in Birmingham in 1830. Holyoake was employed at an early age operating machinery for a Birmingham button-manufacturer; at the same time he attended classes at the Mechanics' Institution:

By the time I was thirteen or fourteen I made a small bright steel fire-grate, with all the improvements then known, as a chimney ornament for my mother. All the drilling in the foundry was done by hand: as this was very laborious, I devised a perpendicular drill to be worked by mill power. At that time I had never seen one. My delight was in mechanical contrivance. Not being able to buy mathematical instruments, I made two pairs of compasses for pencil and pen – one with double point and slide, hammered out of bits of sheet iron. My tutor being pleased with them caused them to be laid on the table at the annual distribution of prizes of the Mechanics' Institution. This led to my being publicly presented with a proper case of mathematical instruments, given by Mr Isaac Pitman, the inventor of phonography. Mr Lloyd, a banker in Birmingham, caused George Stephenson, one night when he was at the House of Commons, to put my name down on his list, though nothing came of it, Mr Lloyd having probably no opportunity of again calling the attention of the famous engineer to it: and I had no other friend in communication with him. What a different career mine had been had I been called up!

Mechanical employment seems to me far preferable to any other open to men in cities. Had there been in my time means of higher education in evening classes, when degrees could be won without University attendance – impossible to me – I should have remained in the workshop. There is more independence in pursuits of handicraft, and more time for original thought, than in clerkship or business. That which made me desirous of escaping from the workshop was the hopelessness of sufficient and certain wages, and the idea of personal subjection associated with it.

George Jacob Holyoake, *Sixty Years of an Agitator's Life* (1892), Vol. I, Ch. 6.

Holyoake's testimony is interesting in a number of ways. In recording his own enthusiasm for invention and mechanical ingenuity it shows how, even in a subordinate position in an obscure Birmingham workshop, those talents found opportunity for fulfilment that would not have been available outside the industrial context. It reveals too, by its reference to a chain of association leading to the House of Commons itself, an apparent democratisation of access: the unknown working boy is brought to the attention of powerful and influential figures. But, in fact, those opportunities turn out to be illusory, and Holyoake concludes by indicating his frustration at the constraints of his personal circumstances, and his inevitable sense of injustice. His life might indeed have turned out differently, but the title of his autobiography indicates the course it actually took. Where Elliott's poem endorses uncritically the idea of working-class intellectualism integrated with industrial labour, Holyoake indicates the dilemma that is inherent in working-class culture generally: does the impulse towards self-improvement lead the talented individual to support a system that seems to promise him real opportunity, or does his sense of its inherent injustice lead him to oppose it? The problem is one which is reflected throughout Chartist autobiography: the lives of figures like Thomas Cooper (*The Life of Thomas Cooper, written by himself*, 1872), William Lovett (*The Life and Struggles of William Lovett*, 1876) and Holyoake himself all reflect a similar pattern of eager and precocious self-education, followed by working experience, leading on the one hand to the education of others, and on the other to the kind of political activism which led to periods of imprisonment.

Institutional provision for working-class culture reflects the conflicts experienced at an individual level. As we have seen in Chapter 3, p.107, genuine working-class involvement with the institutions established for the working-class by middle-class idealism, like the Mechanics' Institutions, was at best limited, and compromised by their function as agencies of social control. At the same time, however, there existed a vigorous and often directly opposed tradition of self-generated intellectual and cultural activity on the part of the working-class, which found expression in a whole range of organisations, societies and publishing ventures, sometimes involving direct confrontation with the law. Both strands have their origin in eighteenth-century enlightenment, reflecting its educational and predominantly scientific impulses: the difference in dimension is, above all, political: whereas the institutions of the establishment invariably specifically proscribed political education, for the self-generating tradition it was an inevitable dimension of self-improvement.

Since the earliest days of the Industrial Revolution working men had taken responsibility for their own education, and the growth of the cities, with their concentrations of working-class population, inevitably accelerated the process. From the 1790s an extensive network of Corresponding Societies, Hampden Clubs and working men's Sunday Schools had developed. Samuel Bamford gives an account of the process, illustrated by his own experience, as it manifested itself in the context of the political unrest of the second decade of the century:

> Instead of riots and destruction of property, Hampden clubs were now established in many of our large towns, and the villages and districts around them; Cobbett's books were printed in a cheap form, the labourers read them, and thenceforward became deliberate and systematic in their proceedings. Nor were there wanting men of their own class, to encourage and direct the new converts; the Sunday Schools of the preceding thirty years, had produced many working men of sufficient talent to become readers, writers,

and speakers in the village meetings for parliamentary reform; some also were found to possess a rude poetic talent, which rendered their effusions popular, and bestowed an additional charm on their assemblages, and by such various means, anxious listeners at first, and then zealous proselytes, were drawn from the cottages of quiet nooks and dingles, to the weekly readings and discussions of the Hampden clubs.

One of these clubs was established in 1816, at the small town of Middleton, near Manchester; and I, having been instrumental in its formation; a tolerable reader also, and a rather expert writer, was chosen secretary. The club prospered; the number of members increased; the funds raised by contributions of a penny a week became more than sufficient for all out goings; and taking a bold step, we soon rented a chapel which had been given up by a society of Kilhamite Methodists. This place we threw open for the religious worship of all sects and parties, and there we held our meetings on the evenings of Monday and Saturday each week. The proceedings of our society; its place of meeting – singular as being the first place of worship occupied by reformers, (for so in those days we were termed) together with the services of religion connected with us – drew a considerable share of public attention to our transactions, and obtained for the leaders some notoriety.

> Samuel Bamford, *Passages in the Life of a Radical* (1884), Ch. 2.

Bamford's account identifies a number of important factors. His club is founded at a point of transition between a rural and an urban culture: its members come from the villages, but Middleton itself is close to Manchester and, as he goes on to record, 'several meetings of delegates from the surrounding districts were held at our chapel, on which occasions the leading reformers of Lancashire were generally seen together'. There is thus both a strong sense of community and a high level of organisation. Educational priorities predominate, but these men are already proficient at reading, writing and public speaking. The reference to the publication of cheap editions of Cobbett hints at another expression of self-generating working-class culture, the development of an alternative publishing tradition which provided for the dissemination of radical material in the form not only of the classic texts of political dissent, but of pamphlets, journals and newspapers. The choice of venue – a Methodist chapel – testifies to the strong connections with dissenting religious practice, but sectarianism itself is rejected in the greater interest of community, and the ultimate dimension is directly political.

The cultural institutions and activities of succeeding generations reflect their origins in the activism of the early years of the nineteenth century. In the early 1840s George Holyoake, to whom a successful career in industry once seemed to be promised, became 'an accredited lecturer of the "Socialist" movement' and an Owenite 'Social Missionary', walking mile after mile to deliver his lectures to audiences of working men in the industrial towns of the West Riding; 'The journey to Huddersfield,' he says at one point, 'was thirty miles, and nearing the town I found my mind, which had been alert on setting out, had become limp.' (Holyoake, op. cit., Vol. I, Ch. 26.) Another working-class auto-didact, Thomas Cooper, gives a fascinating account of his activities in Leicester at the same point in time. Invited to manage a local newspaper, he loses his position as a consequence of contributing to the Chartists' 'penny-paper'. Then, 'in a day or two a deputation from the Chartist committee came to offer me thirty shillings a week, if I would stay in Leicester to conduct their little paper'; at the same time he has plans to give courses of lectures:

> The day after they had sent to ask me to conduct their paper, I had said to one of the Chartist Committee, 'Cannot I have a meeting in your little room at All Saints' Open, next Sunday evening, that I may address your members?'
> 'I am sure we shall all be glad to hear you,' said he.
> And so, having respect to the day, I spoke to them for an hour, partly on a religious theme, and partly

on their sufferings and wrongs, and on the question of their political rights. I offered a prayer – it was the prayer of my heart – at the beginning and close of the meeting. This was in March, and I held these Sunday night meetings in the little room till the stirring events of the spring and summer of that year, 1841, compelled us to seek a much larger arena for our enterprise.

The working men paid me thirty shillings for the first week; but could only raise half the sum the second week. I found they were also in debt for paper. So I proposed that they gave up their periodical to me entirely, and I would father their little debt. I obtained twenty pounds of a friend whom I must not name, and made an engagement with Albert Cockshaw, the printer, to print the *Midland Counties Illuminator* on larger and better paper, and with better type. And I also took a front room in the High Street, as an office for my paper. The Chartists soon elected me their secretary; and a great number of them urged me to make my new place in the High Street a shop for the sale of newspapers – saying they would take their weekly *Northern Star* of me. So I sold not only the Chartist *Northern Star*, but papers and pamphlets of various kinds, and my little shop became the daily *rendezvous* of working men.

Thomas Cooper, *The Life of Thomas Cooper,*
written by himself (1872), Ch. 14.

Cooper's twin roles of lecturer and publisher are typical of this strand of working-class culture, as too are the risks to which they exposed him. Constantly at odds with the law, he is invariably searching for a new lecture hall or devising a new title. By contrast Holyoake's Owenite activities are more organised. There was, in fact, an extensive series of working-class associations – Union Societies, Friendly Societies, Co-operatives Societies and Owenite branches – which covered the full range of the radical spectrum in the 1830s and '40s, and which testify to the capacity of the working class to organise themselves in their own interests. The question must remain as to just how deeply these cultural manifestations penetrated the mass of the urban working class: even their contemporary apologists would seem to concede that reservation. Julius Harney, editor of the Chartist journal, the *Red Republican*, was explicit on this issue:

> Undoubtedly the working-classes are far from faultless. Ignorance, servility, and a want of self-respect are too widely visible, and a state of apathy in respect of their rights and interests, even amongst those who see through the villainy of the present system, are evils [sic] deplored by their true friends.
>
> *Red Republican*, 5 October 1850

But there can be no doubt that the organised societies of the industrial working class provided their members with political education, and with a sense of class awareness and a commitment to community values that found expression not only through the austerities of self-education but through a generally convivial sense of solidarity. Both factors are apparent in this description of the activities of Chartists' organisations and Owenites in Manchester in the 1840s in an extended footnote in Faucher's *Manchester in 1844*:

> As closely connected with the state of religion in Manchester, we may mention 'Carpenter's Hall', and the 'Hall of Science'. The first is the Sunday resort of the Chartists. They open and close their meetings with the singing of democratic hymns, and their sermons are political discourses on the justice of democracy and the necessity for obtaining the charter. The second is an immense building in Camp Field, raised exclusively by the savings of the mechanics and artisans, at a cost of £7,000, and which contains a lecture-hall – the finest and most spacious in the town. It is tenanted by the disciples of Mr Owen. In addition to Sunday lectures upon the doctrines of Socialism, they possess a day and Sunday-school, and increase the number of their adherents by oratorios and festivals – by rural

excursions, and by providing cheap and innocent recreation for the working classes. Their speculative doctrines aim at the destruction of all belief in revealed religion, and the establishment of community of property; and they are vigorously opposed by the evangelical portion of the religious public. It is at the same time admitted, that they have done much to refine the habits of the working classes . . . The large sums of money they raise, prove that they belong to the wealthier portion of the working classes. Their audiences on Sunday evenings are generally crowded.

Manchester in 1844, p. 25n.

If this account confirms the somewhat exclusive nature of this kind of activity, it nevertheless indicates working-class capacity for self-organisation. The Owenite Halls of Science which were established in a number of towns and cities at this time provided for their adherents the satisfaction of participation in a cultural institution organised by themselves and according to their own priorities. They also conceded far more to the rights of their women members to participate in their activities than any other comparable organisations, while their functions were not always perhaps as constrained as Faucher's editor suggests. Here an enthusiast – it is not clear of which sex – describes the climax of the celebrations at an Owenite festival, again in Manchester:

The trumpet was sounded, and the friends collected near our standard, which was a splendid green flag, near which were placed the musicians. There could not be less than one thousand persons assembled. After forming a large circle, we commenced by singing the first festival song, 'O may this feast increase the union of the heart', which was sung with high spirit and delight. A short address was then given and immediately afterwards the dancing began, and hundreds mingled in the mazes of the whirling dance, with such manifestations of innocent joyousness, as might have thawed the heart of the coldest misanthrope.

> *The New Moral World*, 8 June 1839, cited by
> Eileen Yeo, 'Robert Owen and Radical Culture',
> in S. Pollard and J. Salt, eds, *Robert Owen,*
> *Prophet of the Poor* (1971), p.100.

The address was short and the dancing apparently long: it is an attractive insight into the capacity of the urban working class to provide for their own pleasures in an environment that all too often offered them only misery and distress.

Leisure and Entertainment

In *Rural Rides* William Cobbett inveighed against the advocates of the new work ethic:

> The Scotch *feelosofers*, who seem all to have been, by nature, formed for negro-drivers, have an insuperable objection to all those establishments and customs which occasion *holidays*. They call them a *great hindrance*, a great *bar to industry*, a great *draw-back from 'national wealth'*. I wish each of these unfeeling fellows had a spade put into his hand for ten days, and that he were compelled to dig only just as much as one of the common labourers at Fulham. The metaphysical gentleman would, I believe, soon discover the *use of holidays*!
>
> William Cobbett, *Rural Rides* (1830; Penguin
> edn, 1967), p.316.

Given the general conditions of life in the industrial cities in the nineteenth century, it might be thought that those who dwelt within them would have had little opportunity for leisure activity. The pioneer historians of industrial Britain, J. L. and Barbara Hammond, were of this view: they state categorically that the industrial system did not allow for anything other than unrelieved toil:

> The towns that belonged to this age are steeped in

its character; they are one aspect of an industrial system that refused to recognise that the mass of mankind had any business with education, recreation, or the wide and spiritual interests and purposes of life. The age that regarded men, women, and children as hands for feeding the machines of the new industry had no use for libraries, galleries, playgrounds, or any of the forms in which space and beauty can bring comfort or nourishment to the human mind. The new towns were built for a race that was allowed no leisure.

J. L. and Barbara Hammond, *The Skilled Labourer, 1760–1832* (1920), p.7.

The Hammonds are writing of the earlier stages of industrial development but, as we have seen, even at that point in time the situation was more complicated than they suggest. As the century progressed, a heightened civic consciousness was to provide for cultural amenities within the cities; furthermore, while working hours were long and arduous, the existence of a definable working-class culture indicates that social activity beyond the confines of the work-place was by no means unusual. The existence of such possibilities, however, must not obscure the fact that for large numbers of people living in the industrial cities in the nineteenth century – and, in particular, for that sub-working class sector of society whose members appear simply as statistics in the official reports and who rarely find their way into literary record – life was indeed nasty, brutish and short. Throughout this study we have found that the very process of writing about life in the cities has the effect of civilising it: even the sources themselves give only a hint of the unremitting hardship of life at the lowest levels of industrial society.

For the industrial worker the most immediate opportunity for relief came through alcohol. Traditionally inns and public houses had provided meeting places for the working community and, given that alcohol was the safest form of drink in the early nineteenth century, they could be said to provide a social service. But the gin-shops and beer-houses which sprang up in the cities, particularly after the passing of the Beer Act of 1830, were of a very different order. James Kay records the impact of the proliferation of these outlets in Manchester in the early 1830s:

> The decency of our towns is violated, even in this respect, that every street blazons forth the invitations of these haunts of crime. Gin shops and beer houses encouraged by the law (which seems to value rather the amount of the public revenue, than the prevalence of private virtue) and taverns, over which the police can at present exercise but imperfect control, have multiplied with such rapidity that they will excite the strong remonstrances which every lover of good order is prepared to make with government, against the permission, much less the sanction, of such public enormities.
>
> *The Moral and Physical Condition of the Working Classes*, pp.59–60.

It is no coincidence that, reinforced by Evangelical and in particular Dissenting enthusiasm, the temperance movement began at this time, and that its strongholds lay in the towns and cities of the industrial north. The first Temperance Society in England was founded at Bradford in 1830, while Preston, where the total abstinence movement was founded in 1832, was to become known amongst enthusiasts as the 'Jerusalem of teetotalers'.

It is misleading, however, to interpret the condition of life in the cities entirely in negative terms. In support of their position the Hammonds cite Kay, reporting in 1833 on the specific issue of leisure opportunity:

> At present, the entire labouring population of Manchester is without any season of recreation, and is ignorant of all amusements, excepting that very small portion which frequents the theatre. Healthful exercise in the open air is seldom or never taken by the

artisans of this town, and their health certainly suffers considerable depression from this deprivation.

Kay, cit. J. L. and Barbara Hammond, *The Age of the Chartists, 1832–1854* (1930), p.119.

Mrs Gaskell, however, tells a different story. *Mary Barton* begins with a group of working people returning from a day's outing – 'I do not know whether it was on a holiday granted by the masters or a holiday seized in right of nature . . . by the workmen', she writes (*Mary Barton*, Ch. 1). In another of her Manchester stories of the same period, 'Libbie Marsh's Three Eras', she describes the pleasure taken by the workers on their Whitsun Bank Holiday, when they go out into the Cheshire countryside to escape the pressures of their urban existence. They travel from the centre of the city by canal-boat:

> Away the boat went, to make room for others; for every conveyance, both by land and water, is in requisition in Whitsun-week, to give the hard-worked crowds the opportunity of enjoying the charms of the country. Even every standing-place in the canal packets was occupied, and, as they glided along, the banks were lined with people, who seemed to find it object enough to watch the boats go by, packed close and full with happy beings brimming with anticipation of a day's pleasure. The country through which they passed is as uninteresting as can be imagined; but still it is the country; and the screams of delight from the children, and the low laughs of pleasure from the parents, at every blossoming tree that trailed its wreath against some cottage wall, or at the tufts of late primroses which lingered in the cool depths of grass along the river banks; the thorough relish of every-thing, as if dreading to let the least circumstance of this happy day pass over without its due appreciation, made the time seem all too short, although it took two hours to arrive at a place only eight miles from Manchester.

Elizabeth Gaskell, 'Libbie Marsh's Three Eras'
(1847) *The Works of Mrs Gaskell*, ed. A. W.
Ward (The 'Knutsford' Edition, 1906), Vol. I,
p.473.

From their country retreat the workers look back on
'Manchester – ugly, smoky Manchester; dear busy, earnest,
noble-working Manchester; where their children had been
born, and where, perhaps, some lay buried; where their
homes were, and where God had cast their lives, and told
them to work out their destiny.' (p.477.) Distance would
seem to lend enchantment to the view. But notwithstanding
the element of idealisation, the existence of such holiday
opportunity, with the relief that it brought to lives conditioned
almost entirely by the demands of work, is not a figment of
fictional imagination: we can find similar experiences
described in the autobiographical essays of writers like Ben
Brierley and Edwin Waugh, both of them Manchester contemporaries of the novelist.

The Whitsuntide holiday of the workers in Mrs Gaskell's
story is a reminder that the traditional festivals of an earlier
age survived the advance of industrialism. In Ben Brierley's
essay 'A Lancashire Wakes' he begins with a reference to the
holidays of the Christian year, but continues:

> But of all the pastimes the one most dear to me was
> the Wakes, or Rushbearing, which took place annually,
> as far as Hazelworth was concerned, in August. It was
> regarded more particularly as a time of merry-making
> than any other in our village calendar.

Ben Brierley, *Daisy Nook Sketches* (1867, Popular
Edition, 1882), p.222.

Brierley here looks back to the early years of the century, at
a time when all the Lancashire villages celebrated a similar
feast, but as the villages became industrial towns the Wakes
tradition endured, providing the precedent for an annual
holiday. At the same time, however, village bucolics could
be transformed into a cruder brutality. The circus impresario,
'Lord' George Sanger, gives a horrifying account of his

experience when his circus went to the industrial town of Stalybridge for the Wakes holiday:

> I must get on with my story, the next scene of which lies at Stalybridge Wakes, where we found ourselves nearly penniless. The wakes were very rough affairs in those days, the Lancashire lads and lasses making holiday at them in the wildest possible fashion.
>
> Rows were frequent, and now and again terrible scenes were enacted, men and women being literally kicked to fragments by the formidable iron-tipped clogs which formed the general foot-wear. Lancashire men in those days gave very little attention to the use of their fists. The clog was their weapon, and they considered there was nothing unmanly in kicking and biting to death – for they would use their teeth like dogs – any person who had the misfortune to incur their anger.
>
> There was a callous brutality about a Lancashire mob in those days that, looking back, now strikes one as simply appalling. At the very wakes of which I am now speaking we were afforded a shocking example of it.
>
> Nearly opposite our show was a large ginger-bread stall kept by a man whose name I am almost sure was Sheppard, a big, good-humoured fellow, and a well-known fairgoer. I was on the platform with John outside our show just getting ready to call the people up when we noticed a row at Sheppard's ginger-bread stall.
>
> He seemed to be expostulating with a crowd of miners about something, when all at once over went his stall, and the next minute he himself was under their feet with all of them kicking at him anywhere and as hard as they could. From our position on the platform we could see the poor fellow's body with the heavy clogs battered into it as though it was a stuffed sack instead of a human thing.
>
> I wanted to go down to interfere, but John held me back, saying, 'It's no use, boy! They'd only serve you

the same!' And so they would have done, I have no
doubt. At any rate, though the crowd formed a sort
of ring, nobody stirred a hand to save the man who
was being kicked to pulp in the centre of it.

'Lord' George Sanger, *Seventy Years a Showman*
(1910, reprinted, ed. K. Grahame, 1952),
pp.169–70.

Sanger's account of his working life is a useful corrective to
the tendency of more literary reminiscences to sentimentalise
about the values of the popular tradition. At the same time
his book testifies to the vitality of the popular entertaining
arts, and to the demand in the rapidly growing cities for the
kind of spectacle which he provided. After his account of the
Stalybridge affair, he goes on to tell how he met and married
his wife, the daughter of a peep-show proprietor, at the
November fair at Sheffield. Elsewhere he describes wintering
at Liverpool where, 'in the very lowest part . . . I built a
large show, with boarded sides, and a canvas top . . . (where)
. . . we had a semi-dramatic-cum-circus sort of entertainment
that exactly suited the neighbourhood'. (Sanger, op. cit.,
p.204.) Chief amongst this entertainment was a horse-riding
show featuring 'Bill Matthews . . . a good rider, tumbler,
vaulter, and clown'. The year was 1854, the date of the
publication of *Hard Times*, the novel in which Dickens sets
the horse-riders of Sleary's Circus in symbolic contrast
against the ultilitarian bleakness of Coketown. Here Dickens
describes the circus performers, and the kind of entertainment
they provided:

The father of one of the families was in the habit of
balancing the father of another of the families on the
top of a great pole; the father of a third family often
made a pyramid of both of these fathers, with Master
Kidderminster for the apex, and himself for the base;
all the fathers could dance upon rolling casks, stand
upon bottles, catch knives and balls, twirl hand-basins,
ride upon anything, jump over everything, and stick
at nothing. All the mothers could (and did) dance,

upon the slack wire and the tight rope, and perform rapid acts on bare-backed steeds; none of them were at all particular in respect of showing their legs; and one of them, alone in a Greek chariot, drove six in hand into every town they came to . . . There was a remarkable gentleness and childishness about these people, a special inaptitude for any kind of sharp practice, and an untiring readiness to help and pity one another, deserving, often, of as much respect, and always of as much generous construction, as the every-day virtues of any class of people in the world.

Hard Times, Bk 1, Ch. 6.

Dickens's lisping Mr Sleary recognises that in the society of Coketown 'People mutht be amuthed'. Ben Brierley describes in another of his essays the sense of liberation he felt when he saw his first theatrical spectacle – 'The Siege of Troy' – at a Manchester fair. 'What blessings,' he writes, 'we thought, as we munched our dinner, were within reach of mankind, and what a happy life those show people must lead.' ('Easter Holidays', *Daisy Nook Sketches*, p.185.) Horse-riding entertainments were one of the most prominent features of the kind of circus that overlapped with popular theatre – hence the term 'Hippodrome' – and Dickens's account in *Hard Times* of the circus community, with its comradeship, its natural discipline and its inherited and instinctive skills, together with the appeal it possessed for working-class audiences, is confirmed by the detail of Sanger's autobiography.

But however durable the popular tradition, and however resourceful its exponents, opportunities for leisure within the industrial cities in the ninteenth century can in reality only have been very limited. With the development of industrialism and the expansion of commerce a utilitarian work-ethic combined with the religious temper of Evangelicalism to create a spirit hostile to the laxity of traditional pursuits. Manifestations of this attitude were the various societies aimed at improving public morality – not only the temperance societies but institutions like the Society for the Suppression of Vice (founded in 1802), the Lord's Day Observance Society

(1832) and, even as late as 1853, the Anti-Tobacco Society. More directly effective as forces of restraint were the twin factors of regular and rigorous working hours and the development of more efficient systems of social control, in particular the new urban police forces, backed up by an authoritarian magistracy. The result of these various pressures in many places was an actual decline in the opportunities afforded to working people for the free enjoyment of leisure as the city authorities became more conscious of their powers. In evidence given to the Children's Employment Commission of 1843 a Sheffield cutler drew attention to this phenomenon, emphasising specifically the consequences of Sabbatarianism and showing also how schemes of municipal improvement in fact tended to operate to the exclusion of the working class:

No manufacturing town in England is worse situated for places for public or healthful recreation than Sheffield. Thirty years ago it had numbers of places as common land where youths and men could have taken exercise at cricket, quoits, football and other exercises . . . Scarce a foot of all these common wastes remain for the enjoyment of the industrial classes. It is true we have a noble cricket-ground, but access to this must be purchased. We have also perhaps as beautiful botanical gardens as any in the kingdom, but these are opened only once or twice a year to the poorer classes, and they are admitted for sixpence each; and hermetically sealed on Sunday . . . the only day when members of the working classes have leisure to enjoy them . . .

To the want of proper places for healthful recreation may be attributed, in a measure, the great increase of crime in this town and neighbourhood. Young people have no resort but the beer or public-house, and generally those of the worst character, for the most respectable houses will not suffer young men to drink in them; and young men of abilities and moral habits often get entangled with associates of the most profligate character.

Appendix, Second Report of the Children's
Employment Commission (Trades and
Manufactures), Parliamentary Papers, 1843, Vol.
XIV, p.491.

This witness praised the benevolence of the Duke of Norfolk,
a local landowner, who had undertaken to set aside land for
a public park which 'will form a promenade for an evening
walk to the mechanic or manufacturer after their labour', and
he concluded:

> I do not know of any regulation that would be more
> useful, and that would improve the health and morals
> of society, than that sufficient space should be appropri-
> ated in the neighbourhood of large towns to admit
> their youth to indulge in healthful and active recreation.

Ibid.

One of the open spaces traditionally available to the Sheffield
public every Sunday was the Duke of Devonshire's estate at
nearby Chatsworth. It was at about this time, in the 1840s,
that, acting upon sabbatarian principles, the Duke withdrew
this facility, but was then obliged to change his mind on
account of the nuisance created by the heavy drinking of
those who now had nothing else to do. (see Hugh Cunningham, *Leisure in the Industrial Revolution* (1980), p.86.)
  For the new urban middle class the opportunities for leisure
provided by their increasing affluence created something of a
problem. For a man like Rylands (see p.113), preoccupied
with his business to the exclusion of all else, leisure could
hardly have been an issue, but for the business families of
mid-Victorian England – and especially for their female
members – new wealth and, with the employment of increasing numbers of domestic servants, more free time, provided
opportunities for non-productive pleasures which conflicted
with the work-ethic that had made them possible in the first
place. To some extent this problem might be solved by
keeping leisure pursuits safely within home surroundings.

Young ladies could be taught the arts of sketching and water-colour painting, as well as to play on the new mass-produced parlour pianos, while amateur theatricals, charades, and a whole variety of parlour games could be devised to divert, in particular, the young. Victorian novels are full of evidence of this kind of activity. At the same time there was an expansion of institutionalised leisure activity within the cities, and this was marked by an inevitable element of social stratification. To take the most obvious example, the history of the theatre in the period shows, at the beginning of the century, a 'classless' audience, entertained by a wide variety of spectacle, from which the middle classes came largely to exclude themselves. Later in the century, notably under the London influence of actor-managers like the Bancrofts and Charles Kean, a more respectable drama began to attract polite audiences back to the theatres, while at about the same time the newly established music halls provided a separate source of entertainment for both the working-class audience and the more raffish elements of the aristocracy. It was at this time too that first cricket and then association football came to be organised as spectator sports within the urban communities: often sponsored by the upper classes, they provided working-class spectators with a strong sense of community identification.

More ambitiously, the problem of leisure could be solved by making it an instrument both of self-improvement and of social cohesion. This was reflected notably in the enthusiasm for exhibitions, both large and small, which was such a prominent feature of Victorian civic culture. The greatest of them, the Crystal Palace Exhibition of 1851, set a precedent for the provincial cities: it had as its full title 'The Great Exhibition of the Works of Industry of All Nations', but it sought to unite all classes in a celebration of primarily national pride in commercial and industrial achievement. In reality such events accepted social divisions as inevitable: the working class could only attend them outside of working hours, while differential prices of admission often reflected class distinctions. The social vision of the Victorians, though, was at its best energetic and all-embracing. We will close this review of leisure opportunity with an account not of a formal occasion, but of a more spontaneous and local event, a vast festival held in Aston Park, Birmingham, in 1856. The objective was to raise funds for the local hospital, and at the same time to persuade the Corporation to buy the park itself as a civic amenity: the immediate result was a great deal of communal pleasure:

> The fête was to be held on the 28th of July. It fell on a Monday. By common consent business was to be suspended. As the day approached, it became obvious, from the enormous demand for tickets, that the attendance would far exceed the expectations of the most sanguine. Another 25,000 tickets were ordered from the printer, by telegraph. The refreshment contractors were advised of the vastly increased number of hungry customers they might expect. Bakers were set to work to provide hundreds of additional loaves. Orders were given for an extra ton or two of sandwiches. Scores more barrels of ale and porter came slowly into the park, where, within fenced enclosures, they were piled, two or three high, in double lines. Crates upon crates of tumblers, earthenware mugs, and plates arrived. Soda water, lemonade and ginger beer were provided in countless grosses, and in fact everything for the comfort and convenience of visitors that the most careful forethought could suggest, was provided in lavish confusion.
>
> At length the day arrived. The weather was delightfully fine. The village of Aston was gaily decorated; the Royal standard floated from the steeple, and the bells chimed out in joyous melody. The quaint Elizabethan gateway to the park was gay with unaccustomed bunting. The sober old Hall had a sudden eruption of colour, such as it had probably never known before. Flags of all colours, and with strange devices met the eye at every turn. Wagon after wagon, laden with comestibles, filed slowly into the park. The rushing to and fro of waiters and other attendants showed that they expected a busy day of it. As noon approached, train after train deposited at the Aston

station hundreds and thousands of gaily-attired Black Country people. Special trains ran from New Street as fast as they could be got in order; all the approaches to the park were crammed with serried lines – three or four abreast – of omnibuses, waggons, cabs, carts, and every other imaginable vehicle; whilst thousands upon thousands of dusty pedestrians jostled each other in the crowded roads. Fast as the ticket and money collectors could pass them through the gates, continuous streams poured on for hours, until at length the number of persons within the grounds exceeded the enormous total of fifty thousands!

The old Hall was thrown open, and hundreds of people strolled through its quaint rooms and noble galleries. The formal gardens were noisy with unaccustomed merriment. From the terrace one looked upon preparations for amusements, and old English games of all descriptions. Platforms for dancing, and pavilions for musicians, stood here and there. Beyond, in the valley, a long range of poles and skeleton forms showed where the fireworks were in preparation. Down in a corner stood a large stack of firewood through which, when lighted, the 'Fire-King' was to pass uninjured. Swings, merry-go-rounds, and Punch and Judy shows were rare attractions for the young; and soon the whole of that enormous assemblage of people, in the sunlight of a glorious July day, seemed to be thoroughly enjoying themselves.

Suddenly, in one corner, there arose a deep-toned murmur, like the sound of the roaring of the waves upon a broken shore. It deepened in tone and increased in volume, until the whole area of the park was filled with this strange sound. It was the noise of laughter, proceeding simultaneously from fifty thousand throats! From a mysterious-looking shed in the valley opposite the terrace, Mr John Inshaw and some of his friends had just launched a balloon, shaped like an enormous pig! Piggy rose majestically over that vast sea of upturned faces, which he seemed to regard with much attention. But at length, apparently disgusted at being so much laughed at, he started off in the direction of Coleshill, and, to the intense amusement of everybody, persisted in travelling tail foremost.

All classes were represented at the fête. Here you might see a group of well-dressed folks from Edgbaston, next some pale-faced miners from the Black Country, and then the nut-brown faces of some agricultural people. All seemed intent upon fun and pleasure, and so, throughout that long summer day, the crowd increased, and every one seemed to be in a state of absolute enjoyment.

E. Edwards, *Personal Recollections of Birmingham and Birmingham Men* (1877), pp.73–5.

Inevitably in this study of the nineteenth-century industrial city we have concentrated upon the human suffering and social division that were, for the majority of the urban population, the realities of urban life. If we conclude with 'the noise of laughter proceeding simultaneously from fifty thousand throats', it is not through any simple wish to restore the balance or to compromise the darker view. When the Aston fête was over, the people of Birmingham returned to homes and to working lives that reflected the reality of a civilisation built upon major inequities of power and personal reward. The extent to which this is so is revealed unmistakably by both the historical and the literary rewards. But what they also reveal are qualities not only of endurance, but of adaptability and resourcefulness amongst the city dwellers themselves.

Chronological Table

In the following table, where events and procedures take place over a number of years, the date given is that of their initiation. Only major works are included in the list of publications, and the dates given refer to the first full-length publication in book form.

Date	Contemporary events	Publications
1819	Peterloo Massacre; Six Acts; Factory Act	
1824	Leeds Mechanics Institution founded; Combination Act	
1825	Stockton and Darlington Railway opened	
1829	Catholic Emancipation Act; Police Act (Metropolitan force in London)	Carlyle, T., *Signs of the Times*
1830	Liverpool and Manchester Railway opened; 'Beer' Act	
1831	First outbreak of cholera in Britain	
1832	Reform Act; Birmingham Town Hall; Sheffield Mechanics Institution founded	Kay, J. P., *The Moral and Physical Condition of the Working Classes*
1833	Factory Act; First government grant for elementary education	
1834	Poor Law Amendment Act	
1835	Municipal Corporations Act	
1836		Pugin, A. W. N., *Contrasts*
1837	Registration of births, marriages and deaths in England and Wales; W. F. Hook, Vicar of Leeds	
1838	London and Birmingham Railway opened	'Fever' Reports (London); Dickens, C., *Oliver Twist*
1839	First Chartist Petition; County Police Act	
1840		Report of the Health of Towns Committee; Carlyle, T., *Chartism*

Date	Contemporary events	Publications
1841	St. George's Hall, Liverpool	
1842	Second Chartist Petition; Mines Act; Act confirming the municipal charters of Birmingham and Manchester	Report on the Sanitary Condition of the Labouring Population (Chadwick)
1843	Factory Education Bill; Royal Commission on the Health of Towns; Birmingham Mechanics Institution founded	Carlyle, T., *Past and Present*
1844	Factory Act; Rochdale Pioneers	First Report of the Health of Towns Commission; Disraeli, B., *Coningsby*
1845	Irish Potato Famine	Second Report of the Royal Commission on the Health of Towns; Engels, F., *Condition of the Working Class in England* (in German); Disraeli, B., *Sybil*
1846	Repeal of the Corn Laws	
1847	Factory Act (Ten Hours)	
1848	Cholera; Public Health Act; Third Chartist Petition; Christian Socialist Movement founded	Dickens, C., *Dombey and Son*; Gaskell, E., *Mary Barton*
1850	Public Libraries Act; Roman Catholic hierarchy restored; First Roman Catholic Bishop of Birmingham	
1851	Great Exhibition; Census – 51% population urban; Common Lodging Houses Act	Mann, H., *Report on Religious Attendance*
1852	Liverpool Public Library; Manchester Public Library	Report on Draining and Sewerage of Towns
1853	Common Lodging Houses Act	Dickens, C., *Bleak House*
1854		Dickens, C., *Hard Times*; Gaskell, E., *North and South*
1856	County and Borough Police Act	
1857	Industrial Schools Act; Liverpool Dock Board established; National Association for the Promotion of Social Science founded; Manchester Art Treasures Exhibition	

Date	Contemporary events	Publications
1848	Leeds Town Hall	
1859		Smiles, S., *Self Help*
1860		Ruskin, J., *Unto this Last*
1861		Eliot, G., *Silas Marner*
1862	Lancashire Cotton Famine	
1865	Birmingham Central Library opened	
1866	Cholera; Sheffield Outrages	Eliot, G., *Felix Holt*
1867	Reform Act; North of England Council for Promoting the Higher Education of Women founded; Manchester Town Hall; Leeds Public Library	
1868	Artisans' and Labourers' Dwellings Act (Torrens); First Trades Union Congress (held in Manchester)	
1869	Royal Sanitary Commission	Arnold, M., *Culture and Anarchy*
1870	Elementary Education Act; First Tramways Act; Death of Dickens	

Bibliography

Place of publication, unless otherwise indicated, London.

Primary Sources

In this section we have included only works upon which we have drawn in compiling this volume. We have indicated the date of first publication in book form in each case and, where it may prove helpful, details of modern reprints.

Official reports, etc. (in chronological order)

Hansard, Vol. XXVIII 22 May to 26 June 1835
Report of the Select Committee on the Health of Large Towns and Populous Districts, Parliamentary Papers (1840) Vol. XI
Report on the Sanitary Condition of the Labouring Population of Great Britain (Chadwick's Report) 1842 (reprinted, ed. M. W. Flinn, Edinburgh, 1965)
Hansard, Vol. LXVII 28 February to 24 March 1843
Second Report of the Children's Employment Commission (Trades and Manufactures); Appendix, with Reports and Evidence from Sub-Commissioners, Parliamentary Papers 1843, Vol. XIV
Supplementary Report on the Results of a Special Inquiry into the Practice of Interment in Towns, Parliamentary Papers (1843) Vol. XII
Second Report of the Commissioners for Inquiring into the State of Large Towns and Populous Districts, Parliamentary Papers (1845) Vol. XVIII
Second Report of the Royal Sanitary Commission, Parliamentary Papers (1871) Vol. XXXV

Books and other printed sources

Acton, William, *Prostitution* (1857; reprinted, ed. Peter Fryer, 1968)
Ainsworth, William Harrison, *Mervyn Clitheroe* (1858)
Alsop, Alfred, *A Cry For Help From the Slums* (Manchester, n.d., [1870])

Alsop, Alfred, *Lombard Street and How We Got There* (Manchester, n.d., [1870])

Architectural Magazine and Journal, Vol. I (1834)

Arnold, Matthew, *Culture and Anarchy* (1869)

Baines, Edward, *History of the County Palatine of Lancaster* 5 vols. (1831)

Bamford, Samuel, *Passages in the Life of a Radical* (1884, Oxford Paperback edn. 1984)

Bell, Lady, *At the Works* (1907)

Bent, James, *Criminal Life: Reminiscences of Forty-Two Years as a Police Officer* (Manchester, 1891)

Brierley, Ben, *Daisy Nook Sketches* (Manchester, 1867; Popular Edition, 1882)

Brierley, Ben, *Tales and Sketches of Lancashire Life* 9 vols. (Manchester, 1882–6)

Builder, The Vol. I 1844

Burnley, James, *The Romance of Modern Industry* (1889)

Butler, Josephine (ed.), *Woman's Work and Woman's Culture* (1869)

Caminada, Jerome, *Twenty-Five Years of Detective Life* 2 vols. (Manchester, 1895–1901)

Carlyle, Thomas, *Chartism* (1840)

Carlyle, Thomas, 'Corn-Law Rhymes', *Edinburgh Review* (July 1832)

Carlyle, Thomas, *Past and Present* (1843)

Carlyle, Thomas, 'Signs of the Times', *Edinburgh Review* (June 1829)

Carpenter, Mary, 'On the Relation of Ragged Schools to the Educational Movement', *Transactions of the National Association for the Promotion of Social Science* (1857)

Cleaver, Thomas, *'Night' and Other Poems* (1848)

Cobbett, William, *Rural Rides* (1830; Penguin edn, ed. G. Woodcock, Harmondsworth; 1967)

Coleridge, Hartley, *Complete Poetical Works*, ed. Ramsay Colles (1908)

Cooper, Thomas, *The Life of Thomas Cooper, written by himself* (London, 1872; reprinted Leicester, 1971)

De Tocqueville, Alexis, *Journeys to England and Ireland*, trans. George Lawrence and K. P. Mayer, ed. J. P. Mayer (1958)

Dickens, Charles, *Bleak House* (1853)

Dickens, Charles, *Dombey and Son* (1848)

Dickens, Charles, *Hard Times* (1854)

Dickens, Charles, *Martin Chuzzlewit* (1844)

Dickens, Charles, *The Old Curiosity Shop* (1841)
Dickens, Charles, *Oliver Twist* (1838)
Dickens, Charles, *Pickwick Papers* (1837)
Disraeli, Benjamin, *Coningsby* (1844)
Disraeli, Benjamin, *Sybil* (1845)
Economist, The, Vol. V, No. 224 (11 December 1847)
Edwards, E., *Personal Recollections of Birmingham and Birmingham Men* (Birmingham, 1877)
Eliot, George, *Felix Holt, The Radical* (1866)
Eliot, George, *Silas Marner* (1861)
Elliott, Ebenezer, *Poetical Works* (Edinburgh, 1841)
Engels, Friedrich, *The Condition of the Working Class in England in 1844* (Leipzig, 1845; trans. and ed. W. O. Henderson and W. H. Chaloner, Oxford, 1958)
Factory Education Bill of 1843: Six Pamphlets, The (reprinted New York, 1972)
Faucher, Leon, *Manchester in 1844* (London and Manchester, 1844; reprinted 1969)
Gaskell, Elizabeth C., 'Libbie Marsh's Three Eras' (1847); reprinted in Volume One of *The Works of Mrs Gaskell*, ed. A. W. Ward, 8 vols, 'The Knutsford Edition' (1906)
Gaskell, Elizabeth C., *Mary Barton* (1848)
Gaskell, Elizabeth C., *North and South* (1855)
Gaskell, Peter, *The Manufacturing Population of England* (1833; reprinted New York, 1974)
Green, Thomas, 'The Mortality of Birmingham Compared with that of Seven Other Towns', *Transactions of the National Association for the Promotion of Social Science* (1857)
Hawthorne, Nathaniel, *The English Notebooks*, ed. Randall Stewart (New York, 1962)
Hill, Frederic, *Crime: Its Amount, Causes and Remedies* (1853)
Holyoake, George Jacob, *Sixty Years of an Agitator's Life*, 2 vols. (1892)
Hopkins, Gerard Manley, *Selected Prose* ed. Gerald Roberts (1980)
Hopkinson, James, *The Memoirs of James Hopkinson, 1819–1894*, ed. J. B. Goodman (1968)
Horton, Harry H., *Birmingham: A Poem* (Birmingham, 1851; 2nd edn. 1853)
Household Words, Vol. I (1850)
Howson, John S., 'Report on Popular Education in Liverpool', *Transactions of the National Association for the Promotion of Social Science* (1859)
Hudson, J. W., *The History of Adult Education* (1851)

Junior, Junius, *Life in the Low Parts of Manchester: A Midnight Visit to the Thieves and Common Lodging Houses About the City* (Manchester, n.d. [1869])

Kay, James, *The Moral and Physical Condition of the Working Classes Employed in the Cotton Manufacture in Manchester* (1832; reprinted Manchester, 1969)

Kingsley, Frances Emily, *Charles Kingsley: His Letters and Memories of His Life*, 2 vols. (1877)

Leeds Intelligencer, 11 September 1858

Love, Benjamin, *Manchester As It Is* (Manchester, 1839)

Lovett, William, *The Life and Struggles of William Lovett* (1876, reprinted with Preface by R. H. Tawney, 1967)

Mackay, Charles, *Town Lyrics and Other Poems* (1848)

McCulloch, J. R., *A Descriptive and Statistical Account of the British Empire*, 4th edn. (1854)

Melville, Herman, *Redburn* (New York, 1849)

Miall, Edward, *The British Churches in Relation to the British People* (1849)

Newman, John Henry, *Lectures on the Present Position of Catholics* (5th edn 1852)

Newman, John Henry, *Sermons Preached on Various Occasions* (1881; 6th edn, 1887)

Northern Star, The, 2 June 1838

'Old Potter, An', *When I was a Child* (1903; reprinted 1977)

Politics for the People, 27 May 1848, No. 4

Porter, G. R., *The Progress of the Nation* (1847; new edn, 1851)

Prince, J. C., *Hours with the Muses* (1841)

Pugin, A. W. N., *Contrasts* (1836)

Reach, Angus Bethune, *Manchester and the Textile Districts in 1849*, ed. C. Aspin (Helmshore, 1972)

Reade, Charles, *Put Yourself in His Place* (1866)

Red Republican, The, 5 October 1850

Reid, J. Wemyss, *A Memoir of John Deakin Heaton, M. D. of Leeds* (1883)

Ruskin, John, *The Crown of Wild Olive* (1866)

Sanger, 'Lord' George, *Seventy Years a Showman* (1910; reprinted ed. K. Grahame, 1952)

Shaw, Charles, see 'Old Potter, An'

[Shimmin, Hugh], *Pen and Ink Sketches of Liverpool Town Councillors* (Liverpool, 1866)

Stephens, W. R. W., *The Life and Letters of Walter Farquhar Hook*, 2 vols (1878)

Stranger in Liverpool, The (Liverpool, 1823)

Stretton, Hesba, *Jessica's First Prayer* (1866)
Taine, Hippolyte, *Notes on England*, trans., Edward Hyams (1957)
Taylor, W. Cooke, *Notes of a Tour in the Manufacturing Districts of Lancashire* (1842; reprinted with Introduction by W. H. Chaloner, 1968)
The Times, 1 August 1854
Wordsworth, William, *The Excursion* (1814)

Secondary Sources

In this section we list a selection of works of both general and specific interest. In making our selection we have been guided by the priorities established in our text: we would not pretend to have attempted a comprehensive coverage of the secondary literature of our subject.

Archer, J. (ed.), *Art and Architecture in Victorian Manchester* (Manchester, 1985)
Ashton, T. S., *Economic and Social Investigation in Manchester, 1833–1933* (1934)
Bailey, P., *Leisure and Class in Victorian England* (1978)
Binfield, C., *So Down To Prayers: Studies in English Non-Conformity 1790–1920* (1977)
Briggs, Asa, *A History of Birmingham*, Vol. 2: 1865–1938 (1952)
Briggs, Asa, *Victorian Cities* (1963; Pelican edn, 1968)
Chadwick, G. F., *The Park and the Town: Public Landscape in the Nineteenth Century* (1966)
Clarke, B. F., *Church Builders of the Nineteenth Century* (1969)
Cunningham, C., *Victorian and Edwardian Town Halls* (1981)
Cunningham, Hugh, *Leisure in the Industrial Revolution* (1980)
Dennis, Richard J., *English Industrial Cities of the Nineteenth Century* (1984)
Dyos, H. J., *Exploring the Urban Past* (1982)
Dyos, H. J. (ed.), *The Study of Urban History* (1968)
Dyos, H. J. and Wolff, Michael, *The Victorian City: Images and Realities*, 2 vols. (1973)
Fielding, K. J. (ed.), *The Speeches of Charles Dickens* (Oxford, 1960)
Flindall, R. P. (ed.), *The Church of England, 1815–1948* (1972)
Fraser, D. (ed.), *A History of Modern Leeds* (Manchester, 1980)
Furneaux Jordan, R., *Victorian Architecture* (Harmondsworth, 1966)

Gilbert, A. D., *Religion and Society in Industrial England* (1976)
Gill, C., *History of Birmingham*, Vol. 1, to 1865 (1952)
Hammond, J. L. and Barbara, *The Age of the Chartists, 1832–54* (1930)
Hammond, J. L. and Barbara, *The Skilled Labourer, 1760–1832* (1920)
Hammond, J. L. and Barbara, *The Town Labourer* (1917)
Harrison, J. F. C., *The Early Victorians, 1832–51* (1971)
Hollingworth, B. (ed.), *Songs of the People* (Manchester, 1977)
Hopkins, E., *A Social History of the English Working Classes, 1815–1945* (1979)
Inglis, B., *Poverty and the Industrial Revolution* (1971)
Kellett, J. R., *Railways and Victorian Cities* (1979)
Kidd, A. J. and Roberts, K. W., *City, Class and Culture* (Manchester, 1985)
Macdonagh, O., *Early Victorian Government, 1830–1870* (1977)
Maclure, J. S. (ed.), *Educational Documents, England and Wales 1816–1968* (1965; 2nd edn, rev., 1968)
Maidment, B. (ed.), *The Poorhouse Fugitives* (Manchester, 1987)
Mark, Sir Robert, *In the Office of Constable* (1978)
Mathias, P., *The First Industrial Nation* (1969)
Messinger, G. S., *Manchester in the Victorian Age* (Manchester, 1985)
Muir, R., *A History of Liverpool* (1907)
Mumford, Lewis, *The City in History* (1961; Pelican edn, 1966)
Pahl, R. E., Flynn, R. and Buck, N. H., *Structures and Processes of Urban Life* (1983)
Park, R. and Burgess, E., *The City* (1967)
Pass, A. J., *Thomas Worthington: Victorian Architecture and Social Purpose* (Manchester, 1988)
Perry, P. J., *A Geography of Nineteenth-Century Britain* (1975)
Pike, B., *The Image of the City in Modern Literature* (Princeton, N.J., 1981)
Pike, E. R., *Human Documents of the Industrial Revolution in Britain* (1966)
Pollard, S. and Salt, J. (eds), *Robert Owen, Prophet of the Poor* (1971)
Raven, Jon (ed.), *Victoria's Inferno* (Wolverhampton, 1978)
Raynor, J. and Harris, E., *The Urban Experience* (1977)
Redford, A., *Labour Migration in England 1800–1850* (1926)
Rowell, G., *The Victorian Theatre, 1792–1914* (1956; 2nd edn, 1978)

Simon, B., *The Two Nations and the Educational Structure, 1780–1870* (1974)

Smith, S. M., *The Other Nation* (Oxford, 1980)

Steedman, C., *Policing the Victorian Community* (1984)

Tylecote, M. *The Mechanics Institutes of Lancashire and Yorkshire* (Manchester, 1957)

Vincent, D., *Bread, Knowledge and Freedom* (1981)

Waller, P. J., *Town, City and Nation* (1983)

Walton, M., *Sheffield: Its Story and Its Achievements* (Sheffield, 1948)

Weber, Adna, *The Growth of Cities in the Nineteenth Century* (1899)

Wickham, E. R., *Church and People in an Industrial City* (1957)

Williams, R., *The Country and the City* (1973)

Wolff, J. and Seed, J., *The Culture of Capital: Art, Power and the Nineteenth Century Middle Class* (Manchester, 1988)

Wright, D. G. and Jowitt, J. (eds), *Victorian Bradford* (Bradford, 1982)

Index